Immanuel

SWINDOLL
LEADERSHIP
LIBRARY

Immanuel

JESUS CHRIST:
CORNERSTONE OF OUR FAITH

JOHN A. WITMER

CHARLES R. SWINDOLL, GENERAL EDITOR

WORD PUBLISHING
Nashville•London•Vancouver•Melbourne

IMMANUEL
Swindoll Leadership Library

Published in association with Dallas Theological Seminary (DTS):
General Editor: Dr. Charles R. Swindoll, President
Managing Editor: Dr. Roy B. Zuck

The theological opinions expressed by the author are not necessarily the official position of Dallas Theological Seminary.

Library of Congress Cataloging in Publication Data:

Witmer, John Albert, 1920–
Immanuel : Jesus Christ, cornerstone of our faith /
John Albert Witmer : Charles R. Swindoll, general editor.
p. cm.— (Swindoll leadership library)
Includes bibliographical references and index.

ISBN 0-8499-1369-1 (hardcover : alk. paper)

1. Jesus Christ—Person and offices. I. Swindoll, Charles R.
II. Title.   III. Series.

BT202.W597   1998   98-15085
232–dc21   CIP

Printed in the United States of America
98 99 00 01 02 03 04 05 06 BVG 9 8 7 6 5 4 3 2 1

In memory of my parents,

Albert F. and Mary E. Witmer,

who dedicated me to the service of God before birth
and by personal example and precept guided me
as a child of twelve to saving faith
in the Lord Jesus Christ

Contents

Foreword

ONE OF THE MOST PROFOUND Bible studies ever held took place on a dusty road between Jerusalem and Emmaus. Two discouraged disciples on their way home encountered the resurrected Jesus, but they failed to recognize Him. Unsure, uncertain—certainly unnerved—by recent events in Jerusalem, they had developed a "crisis of faith" as they tried to reconcile what they had seen with what they believed.

Jesus understood their confusion . . . and He offered solid answers from the Word of God. "And beginning with Moses and all the Prophets, he explained to them what was said in all the Scriptures concerning himself" (Luke 24:27). The Bible had the answers to the disciples' questions, and the answers focused on the person and work of Jesus Christ.

Jesus Christ . . . Son of God . . . Messiah . . . Savior . . . the Word . . . Son of Man . . . King of kings and Lord of lords . . . the second person of the Godhead is clearly the central focus in God's drama of redemption. His first coming was so significant that it serves as the dividing line of history for most of the world. And yet, tragically, many Christians know only a small fraction of what the Bible teaches about our Savior and Lord.

John Witmer has done us all a great service by distilling what the Bible teaches about Jesus Christ. Much like a careful archaeologist, John has diligently dug through God's Word and brought to the surface the riches about Jesus Christ found within its pages. Like treasures held up to the light, he allows the various facets of the person and work of Christ to flash their brilliance.

Where was the Son of God before His birth in Bethlehem? What part did God's Son play in the Old Testament? What is He doing now? What will He do in the future? Witmer addresses these and numerous other questions by taking us back to the Word of God for authoritative answers. As Jesus did with the disciples on the road to Emmaus, Witmer has taken us aside in this volume to explain "what was said in all the Scriptures concerning [Jesus]."

Read through this book carefully . . . and prayerfully . . . if you hope to glean the maximum benefit from its pages. Look up the passages of Scripture and allow *all* God's Word to open its treasures to your gaze. As you do, you will respond as the disciples on the road to Emmaus, "Were not our hearts burning within us while he talked with us on the road and opened the Scriptures to us?" (Luke 24:32). You will come away from this study with a deeper love for our Lord and Savior Jesus Christ.

—CHARLES R. SWINDOLL
General Editor

Introduction

Our Lord Jesus Christ is the most important and significant person identified with humanity in this cosmic scene. This excludes, of course, God the Father and God the Holy Spirit, who together with the Lord Jesus—also called "Immanuel," which means, "God with us" (Matt. 1:23; Isa. 7:14)—constitute the eternal triune Godhead. This emphasis on the importance of the Lord Jesus is part of the eternal plan of the triune Godhead for this cosmos from its beginning—the angelic creation—to its consummation—the creation of new heavens and a new earth (Rev. 21:1). God's declared intent is "that in everything he [Jesus] might have the supremacy. For God was pleased to have all his fullness dwell in him, and through him to reconcile to himself all things, whether things on earth or things in heaven, by making peace through his blood, shed on the cross" (Col. 1:18–19; see 1 Cor. 15:27–28). God the Father also desires that the Lord Jesus Christ and His sacrificial death be the focus of faith and commitment for Christians as well.

It is fitting, therefore, that we should study closely what the Bible teaches about the person and work of our Lord Jesus Christ. This involves the totality of the Scriptures, the Old Testament as well as the New, because, as God's angelic messenger told the apostle John, "the testimony of Jesus is the spirit of prophecy" (Rev. 19:10). Many Scriptures make it clear that the existence and ministry of our Lord Jesus Christ did not begin with His birth in human form as the Virgin Mary's baby in Bethlehem (e.g., John 1:14–15, 30; 17:5; Gal. 4:4; Phil. 2:7). He existed eternally as the Word (John 1:1–2), the second person of the Godhead, and was active in preincarnate ministry and revelation in the Old Testament.

Our analysis of the biblical teaching concerning the person and work of Jesus Christ falls into four major divisions: The Preincarnate Word of God, the Incarnate Son of God, the Glorified Christ of God, and the Reigning King of God. In His preincarnate existence and ministry He is called the Word (John 1:1, 14; 1 John 1:1; Rev. 19:13). In His incarnate life and ministry He is frequently called the Son of God (e.g., Matt. 3:17; 14:33; 16:16; 17:5; Mark 1:1; 3:11; 5:7; Luke 1:32, 35; John 1:34, 49; 11:27; 17:1; Rom. 1:3–4; 8:3; 1 Cor. 1:9; 2 Cor. 1:19; Gal. 4:4; 1 Thess. 1:10; Heb. 1:2–3; 4:14; 10:29; 1 John 3:8, 23; 4:9–10, 14; 5:9–13, 20; 2 John 3; Rev. 2:18). In His present ministry He is at the right hand of God the Father in heaven as the glorified Christ (Ps. 110:1; Matt. 22:44; 26:64; Mark 12:36; 14:62; 16:19; Luke 20:42; 22:69; Acts 2:33–36; 5:31; 7:55–56; Rom. 8:34; Eph. 1:20; Col. 3:1; Heb. 1:3, 13; 8:1; 10:12; 12:2; 1 Pet. 3:22). In His future ministry He will reign on earth as "King of kings and Lord of lords" (Rev. 19:16) over the millennial kingdom of righteousness and peace, on the throne of his father David (Luke 1:32–33). These four divisions embrace the person and work of Christ from eternity past to eternity future and all of cosmic time between. That is a subject broad enough and wondrous enough to cause any mere human being to bow in humble adoration and worship before the Lord Jesus.

Colossians 1:15–20 stands as a marvelous capsule statement of Christology—the organized theological discussion of the person and work of Christ. Obviously not all four divisions of this subject are stated in these verses, but its broad scope is outlined, from His participation in cosmic creation as "the image of the invisible God" through the final reconciling to God of "all things, whether things on earth or things in heaven, by making peace through his blood, shed on the cross." This means that finally even Satan and his demonic hosts and all unrepentant human beings will be brought into submission and will be obliged to confess "that Jesus Christ is Lord, to the glory of God the Father" (Phil. 2:11). This includes the judgment of eternal torment in the lake of fire for Satan and his cohorts (Rev. 20:10; 19:20) and all unregenerate human beings (20:11–15).

Part 1

THE PREINCARNATE
WORD OF GOD

———◆———

One

THE WORD OF GOD AS A MEMBER
OF THE TRIUNE GODHEAD

———⊙———

WE USE THE TITLE *Word* in speaking of the preincarnate Lord Jesus Christ because Scripture uses it in John 1:1–5. The identity of the Word with Jesus Christ is stated in verse 14: "The Word became flesh and lived for a while among us. We have seen his glory, the glory of the one and only Son, who came from the Father, full of grace and truth." In fact, John 1:1–5 can serve as that capsule Scripture passage for this first division of our study of Jesus' person and work. It covers His eternal existence, His identity and relationship with God, His participation in the triune Godhead's work of creation, and His involvement with humanity as its source of life ("and that life was the light of men," v. 4). Interestingly the apostle John is the only biblical author who used the title *Word* for Christ (John 1:1, 14; 1 John 1:1; Rev. 19:13).

Through the centuries biblical scholars have wondered why John used this title, especially since he presented it without any explanation, simply stating, "In the beginning was the Word." Many have suggested that it had a meaning well known to his readers. They surmise that John, being a Jew and familiar with the Old Testament, was aware of the gradual personification there of "the word of the LORD" (Ps. 33:4, 6; see Pss. 107:20; 119:89, 105; 147:15, 18) and the wisdom of God (Job 28:12–28; Prov. 1:2–33; 8:1–9:6). This biblical personification of the wisdom of God is carried

1

forward and accentuated by two of the Jewish apocryphal books, the *Wisdom of Jesus ben Sirach* and the *Wisdom of Solomon*.

Numerous scholars also relate John's use of this title to its occurrence in the religious philosophy of the flourishing Alexandrian Jewish colony represented primarily by Philo in A.D. 40–50, who combined his Jewish convictions with strong influences from Greek philosophy into a confusing doctrine of the *logos* (the Greek noun translated "word") that involves God and an intermediary between God and mankind. In effect, Philo personified the divine *logos* but refused to deify him, since to the Jews, God is one in the absolute sense. Bromiley concludes his discussion on Philo by writing, "the logos seems to be a convenient link between the Creator God and the world which he has made."[1]

The teaching concerning the *logos* that Philo borrowed and adapted goes back at least as far as Heraclitus (ca. 525–475 B.C.), who considered the law of change the only thing that does not change, which is the *logos*.[2] This cosmic principle of the *logos* was adapted by the Stoics (200–100 B.C.) who identified Zeus as the universal *Logos*—who is reason, who never changes his mind, and who permeates all things through sparks of divine fire called the *logoi* that control the development of each thing.[3] As with Alexandrian Jewish Hellenism as represented by Philo, the concept of the *logos* in Greek philosophy, despite use of the same Greek word and a few superficial similarities, does not correspond to the apostle John's revelation concerning Christ the eternal Word of God, His incarnation, and His ministry in the past, the present, and the future.

Actually the Greek word *logos*, which was in common usage, refers both to a concept, idea, or inward thought and to the verbal expression, spoken or written, that gives expression to that idea and communicates or reveals it to others. The inward thought remains invisible and unknowable until it is expressed audibly or visibly in a word (*logos*). This is exactly and beautifully the relationship between the first and second persons of the Godhead (John 14:8–11; Col. 1:15; Heb. 1:3a) and undoubtedly is the reason John was led to refer to Christ as "the Word."

Philip Schoff wrote, "John (and he alone) called Christ the 'Logos' of God, *i.e.*, the embodiment of God and the organ of all his revelations. As the human reason or thought is expressed in word, and as the word is the medium of making our thoughts known to others, so God is known to himself and to the world in and through Christ as the personal Word. . . . 'Logos' designates the metaphysical and intellectual relation . . . of Christ to God."[4]

THE WORD OF GOD ETERNAL WITH
GOD THE FATHER AND GOD THE HOLY SPIRIT

The first revelation the apostle John gave concerning the Word is a decla-ration of His eternality—"In the beginning was the Word" (John 1:1a). This statement obviously is designed to remind the reader or listener of the opening sentence of the Bible—"In the beginning God created the heavens and the earth" (Gen. 1:1). In part because of this similarity, Lewis Sperry Chafer spoke of the Gospel of John as the theological beginning of the New Testament. John undoubtedly viewed the word *beginning* in the two passages as referring to the same starting point.

Whether one agrees with John in this identity of the beginning, at what-ever point a person places the beginning of John's statement, at that point "was the Word" (John 1:1). The Word did not come into being at that time; He did not come into being before that time; He simply *was* at that time, eternally existent as God Himself. In your mind's eye you can make a point to mark the beginning of time and of all things except God, and at that point the Word was; in other words, He was eternally existent. John used the imperfect tense of the Greek verb translated "to be," which signi-fies existence at the point mentioned, in this case eternally. To underscore this truth John later stated, "He was with God in the beginning" (1:2), affirming the Word's possession of the same eternality as God.

Although numerous Scriptures speak of Jesus' preexistence before His incarnation (e.g., John 1:14; 3:13, 17; 17:5; Gal. 4:4; Col. 1:15–17, 19; Heb. 1:6; 10:5; 1 John 1:2), they do not automatically teach His eternality. The Jehovah's Witnesses and some other cultists teach that Jesus existed be-fore the Incarnation but deny His eternality, teaching that He was the first creation of God. Few Scriptures besides these in John 1 teach the eternality of the Word of God, and most of those do so only by inference. The clearest is Jesus' own statement, "I tell you the truth . . . before

Abraham was born, I am" (John 8:58). To claim mere preexistence Jesus would have said, "Before Abraham was born, I was." Instead he took God's covenantal name with Israel—"I AM" (Exod. 3:14)—and claimed eternal existence. In addition, Scriptures that equate Jesus' deity with that of God the Father (e.g., Phil. 2:6; Col. 1:15, 19; 2:9; Heb. 1:3) state His eternality by inference because of the eternality of God.

Our finite minds have comparatively little difficulty conceiving of eternity stretching without end into the future. Believers in the Lord Jesus Christ have received eternal life (John 3:16, 36). This signifies primarily spiritual life, a quality of life, the life possessed by God and bestowed by God (17:3); but eternal life also will continue forever—it will never end (6:50–51; 10:28; Rev. 22:5). Scripture also makes it clear that all unregenerate human beings also will exist forever, but in eternal torment, not eternal life; they will be separated from God in the lake of fire (Matt. 25:41, 46; Rev. 20:10–15). That is the horror of dying without trusting the Lord Jesus Christ and receiving the salvation and eternal life provided by God's grace. Awareness of that eternal torment that awaits the unregenerate should spur all Christians to greater personal evangelism and support of evangelistic and missionary agencies.

It is much more difficult, however, for human beings to conceive of eternity past, of existence stretching back into the past without beginning. But this is true of God (Deut. 33:27; Pss. 41:13; 90:2; Isa. 44:6; 48:12; 57:15; Rom. 1:20) and according to John is true of the Word as well. This fact of His self-existence is what the Lord Jesus, the incarnate Word, declared concerning Himself, as stated earlier, when He told the Jews who debated with him, "I tell you the truth, before Abraham was born, I am!" (John 8:58). By this statement Jesus was claiming for Himself exactly what God had claimed when He told Moses, "I AM WHO I AM. This is what you are to say to the Israelites, 'I AM has sent me to you'" (Exod. 3:14). The Jews understood Jesus' claim, because "at this, they picked up stones to stone him" (John 8:59), judging Him guilty of blasphemy.

Logic—some might even say common sense—demands that eternality and self-existence be true of someone or something. It is inconceivable that everything, including God, just suddenly sprang into being out of nothing. In the past, secular scientists have considered matter to be eternal. With the splitting of the atom and other discoveries concerning matter, secular scientists in more recent years have attributed eternality also to energy. However, the scientific law of entropy—the principle that the amount of available energy is always decreasing in a closed system such as our universe—argues against energy being eternal. Through the years Christian scientists have argued for the eternality of God in opposition to atheistic secularism, and in more recent years they have used the latest scientific discoveries to press their insistence that God must be the eternal One.

Logic also demands that the simpler and less complex always be produced by the more complex, not vice versa. That which possesses life and personality is more complex than that which is inanimate and impersonal; therefore, logically, life and personality cannot have been produced from matter or energy. The eternal, self-existent God of the Bible, therefore, is the only logical explanation of all things; He must be the eternal, self-existent One. The apostle John stated that this eternality and self-existence belongs to Jesus Christ, the Word.

EQUALITY OF THE WORD IN FELLOWSHIP
WITH GOD THE FATHER AND GOD THE SPIRIT

John's second statement about the Word in John 1:1 is, "the Word was with God." Most commentators agree that in His eternal existence the Word was in continuous association and fellowship with God. The verb "was" repeats the imperfect tense of the Greek verb translated "to be" in the first clause of this verse. In addition, a number of commentators note that the Greek preposition translated "with," when it occurs with the accusative case of the noun as here, describes the two persons involved as face to face in an equal and close relationship (see 1 John 1:2; 2:1). Vincent summarized the significance of John's statement as follows: "the divine Word not only abode with the Father from all eternity, but was in the living, active relation of communion with Him."[5]

The apostle John's third statement in John 1:1 further emphasizes the equality of the Word with God the Father and God the Holy Spirit: "and the Word was God." Because the Greek word translated "God" *(theos)* has no definite article in the Greek text, the Jehovah's Witnesses, who believe

Jesus is a divine being but not fully and truly God, translate the clause, "and the Word was a god." This is a form of the ancient heresy of Arianism and in effect is a repetition of Philo's error. It is rejected as grammatically unsupportable by such Greek scholars as Henry Alford and A. T. Robertson, who call attention to the parallel construction in Jesus' statement to the Samaritan woman by the well of Sychar: "God is spirit, and his worshipers must worship in spirit and in truth" (John 4:24). Another parallel construction is found in John 1:49, which reads, "you are the King of Israel," where the word translated "king" occurs without the definite article but is properly translated "the king." Concerning this construction E. C. Colwell stated (in what is called Colwell's Rule), "Definite predicate nouns which precede the verb usually lack the article . . . a predicate nominative which precedes the verb cannot be translated as an indefinite or 'qualitative' noun solely because of the absence of the article; if the context suggests that the predicate is definite, it should be translated as a definite noun."[6]

The word *logos,* which has the definite article in all three clauses in John 1:1, is clearly the subject of the first two clauses. It is obviously meant to be the subject of this third clause even though in the Greek word order it follows the word translated "God" *(theos).* Robertson pointed out that in Greek the first position in the sentence or clause, as here, is often given to the predicate "simply because, as a rule, the predicate is the most important thing in the sentence."[7] Here the fact that the Word is God is the most important thing. First position in the clause or sentence is also given frequently for emphasis, which may also be involved here. John undoubtedly wanted his readers to know that the Word truly is God.

Had the article occurred with the word *theos* as well as with *logos* ("the God was the Word") it would have meant that the totality of what constituted God was expressed in the Word, thus denying the doctrine of the Trinity and supporting the ancient heresy of Sabellianism, a form of Modalistic Monarchianism (see page 84). It also would have denied the personal distinctiveness and the relationship between the *logos* and God the Father, stated in the second clause and in verse 2. The clause as stated by John means that the Word *(logos)* possesses the character of God *(theos)* and is God in substance and essence.

As Tenney wrote, "The three statements of v. 1 bring out three different aspects of the nature of the Word. The first speaks of his preexistence, the second of his distinctiveness, and third of his deity."[8] Then in verse 2, in the apostle John's characteristic mode of writing, he repeated two of the ideas from verse 1 for emphasis—the eternal existence of the Word and his eternal face-to-face relationship of fellowship and equality with God. Correctly translated and interpreted, these two verses contribute to the recognition, development, and formulation of the biblical and Christian doctrine of the Trinity. This is the doctrine that the one eternal God of the Bible subsists in a Trinity of Persons—Father, Son (or Word), and Holy Spirit.

The doctrine of the Trinity is a biblical doctrine, not in the sense that it is stated in any one verse of Scripture but in the sense that its recognition and formulation are demanded by a wealth of biblical evidence such as this passage. In this regard 1 John 5:7 as it occurs in the King James Version ("For there are three that bear record in heaven, the Father, the Word, and the Holy Ghost: and these three are one"), though an excellent statement of the doctrine of the Trinity, has no early Greek manuscript support and probably was not in the original letter written by John but inserted later.

On the one hand the Bible clearly teaches that there is one God (Deut. 6:4; 4:35, 39; Rom. 3:30; 1 Cor. 8:4, 6; Eph. 4:6; 1 Tim. 2:5). The Bible also clearly teaches that three persons—God the Father, God the Son, and God the Holy Spirit—possess and utilize the attributes of God, exercise the prerogatives of God such as accepting worship and forgiving sins, and clearly are identified as God. The Bible, therefore, presents God the Father, God the Son, and God the Holy Spirit each as equally and eternally God, constituting the one God, and yet each as a distinct person in fellowship and cooperative activity with each other. As Jesus expressed it to the Jews in Solomon's Colonnade of the temple, "I and the Father are one" (John 10:30). Jesus was not claiming simply unity of goal or interest but unity of nature, as the Jews clearly recognized (10:33). Jesus later expressed a personal interrelationship with God the Father, as seen in His doing the works of God (10:37–38).

Other Trinitarian passages of Scripture include the baptismal formula given by the resurrected Jesus Christ to His disciples at their commissioning before His ascension: "Therefore go and make disciples of all nations, baptizing them in the name [singular] of the Father and of the Son and of the Holy Spirit" (Matt. 28:19). The three persons of the triune Godhead were involved in the annunciation by the angel Gabriel to the Virgin Mary (Luke 1:35), the baptism of Jesus by John the Baptist (Matt. 3:16–17), and Jesus' Upper Room Discourse with His disciples the evening of His arrest (John 14–16). The three persons of the Godhead are joined together in the benediction of 2 Corinthians 13:14, the introduction of 1 Peter 1:2, and the discussions of 1 Corinthians 12:4–6 and Ephesians 4:4–6. Some Old Testament implications of the Trinity include the Aaronic benediction for the sons of Israel (Num. 6:15–16), Jacob's benediction on Joseph's sons (Gen. 48:15–16), and the threefold occurrence of "holy" in Isaiah 6:3. The latter could also be a Hebrew way of expressing emphasis on God's holiness. Much additional biblical evidence could be given in support of the doctrine of the Trinity.

Although the statement of the doctrine of the Trinity is simple—"We worship one God in trinity and trinity in unity without confounding the persons or dividing the substance" (Athanasian Creed)[9] —its explanation and comprehension are difficult, even impossible in the ultimate sense, because it is utterly unique and transcends human earthly experience. Many illustrations of the Trinity can be suggested, such as the human individual composed of body, soul, and spirit. (However, others believe the Bible teaches man consists of only two parts—material and immaterial.) Some like the illustration of an egg, which consists of shell, white, and yolk. This illustration logically breaks down, however, because each part of the egg is only that part of the egg, not the whole egg. Each person of the Trinity, on the other hand, is completely God and at the same time a distinct person from the other two persons. Perhaps the closest natural thing to an illustration of the Trinity is light, which consists of three different kinds of rays and yet forms one light. This is appropriate since the Bible states "God is light" (1 John 1:5), but in the end even this illustration logically breaks down.

In the final analysis all illustrations of the Trinity prove inadequate to fully explain this unique reality. Bernard of Clairvaux wrote, "How can plurality consist with unity, or unity with plurality? To examine the fact closely is rashness, to believe it is piety, to know it is life, and life eternal."[10]

The Puritan divine John Arrowsmith said, "The Trinity is a mystery which my faith embraces as revealed in the Word, but my reason cannot fathom."[11] Once again in this volume a thorough discussion is not appropriate; but I must confess that despite the numerous times I have taught the doctrine of the Trinity as clearly as I could, each time at the end of the course I had to confess to myself and to the class that, although I could explain the doctrine adequately and believe it wholeheartedly, I did not comprehend it in the sense of fathoming its depths of meaning. I take solace in the reputed wry remark attributed to Jonathan Edwards, another Puritan divine, concerning the Trinity: "He who would deny it will lose his soul, and he who would too much seek to understand it will lose his wits."

THE WORD WORKING WITH GOD THE FATHER AND GOD THE SPIRIT

In Creating All Things

The apostle John followed his revelations concerning the person of the Word and His eternal relationship and identity with God (John 1:1–2) with a revelation concerning the involvement of the Word in cosmic creation. He wrote, "Through him all things were made; without him nothing was made that has been made" (1:3). This supports the idea that the "beginning" in verses 1–2 is to be identified with the beginning in Genesis 1:1. Here the tense of the Greek verb translated "were made" (more literally "came into being") presents the creative process in all its complexity and progression. The words "through him" signify the agent of an action. The statement that follows—"without him nothing was made that has been made"—is more than Hebraic antithetical parallelism (the repetition of the same idea in a negative statement). It is a specific denial of the ancient Gnostic heresy of the eternity of matter and of the participation of angels or aeons in the creative process.

John's presentation of our Lord Jesus Christ's involvement as the Word in the creation of all things is supported by other Scriptures. Later in this chapter John wrote, "The world was made through him" (John 1:10). The apostle Paul declared, "For by him all things were created: things in heaven and on earth, visible and invisible, whether thrones or powers or rulers or authorities; all things were created by him and for him" (Col. 1:16). Similarly the writer of the Epistle to the Hebrews described the Son as God's Heir "through whom he made the universe" (Heb. 1:2).

Elsewhere in the Scriptures creation is attributed to God (Gen. 1:1–2:4; Exod. 20:11; Job 38:4; Ps. 90:2; Isa. 44:24; Acts 14:15; Rom. 1:20; Heb. 11:3; Rev. 10:6), understood in most cases to mean God the Father. In a few Scriptures God the Holy Spirit is mentioned as involved in creation (Gen. 1:2; Job 33:4; Ps. 104:30). Also in at least two verses God's Word is said to be His instrument of creation (Ps. 33:6; Heb. 11:3), and frequently creation is described as the result of His speaking (Gen. 1:3, 6, 9, 11, 14, 20, 24, 26; Pss. 33:9). In Proverbs 8:27–31 the wisdom of God is personified and described as involved in creation. Elsewhere wisdom is spoken of as God's instrument in creation (Ps. 136:5; Prov. 3:19; Jer. 10:12; 51:15). The point of this is that Scripture presents God the Father, the Word of God—the Lord Jesus Christ—and the Holy Spirit of God as involved in God's work of creation without specifically identifying the Word or the Holy Spirit as members of the triune Godhead; yet they must be, because creation is God's work. Perhaps the Old Testament verse that best clarifies the Trinity in the work of creation is the statement, "Let us make man in our image, in our likeness" (Gen. 1:26). The first point to notice here is that God is quoted as speaking to Himself, a suggestion of the Trinity's involvement in creation (see 3:22; 11:7; Isa. 6:8). Then there is the use of the plural pronouns "us" and "our." Most Old Testament scholars consider this an example of the "plural of majesty," but these pronouns may well imply God's subsistence in a Trinity of persons in light of other biblical evidence.

A New Testament verse that clearly states the relationship among the members of the Godhead in God's work of creation is 1 Corinthians 8:6. There the apostle Paul emphasized that, in contrast to the false gods represented by the idols worshiped by the pagans, the triune God of the Bible worshiped by Christians is the only true God. This God involves "the Father, from whom all things came and for whom we live; and there is but one Lord, Jesus Christ, through whom all things came and through whom we live." Thus God the Father is identified as the primary source, as well as the goal, of everything, and Jesus Christ, the Word, is identified as the agent of accomplishing everything. This verse is one of the clearest in setting forth the relationship between God the Father and God the Son in the work of creation. It presents what theologians call the "economic order" of the triune Godhead, the relationship among the three members of the Trinity in carrying out all the work of God. In summary, creation is from God the Father through the Lord Jesus Christ (the Word) by means of the Holy Spirit of God.

That Jesus Christ should be the secondary agent of God's creation is appropriate; as the Word He is the person of the Godhead who reveals God and makes Him manifest. Just as a word is an expression of a human person's thoughts, so the Word of God is the expression and manifestation of God. Since Scripture makes it clear that creation is a means of God's revelation of Himself (Ps. 19:1–6; Rom. 1:19–20), it is fitting that the Word of God be involved in it. Likewise, as discussed in chapters 4–7, it is appropriate that the Word is the member of the Godhead who became incarnate (John 1:14) as the Lord Jesus Christ.

In Sustaining All Things

Scripture also indicates that in relation to His creation God is not an absentee landlord. He did not create the universe to abandon it to the operation of inherent principles, the position generally associated with Deism, a view that rose to some prominence in England and in western Europe during the latter seventeenth and eighteenth centuries. It is also the position of secular science with its discovery of supposedly absolute, inviolate laws that control the operation of the universe. To the contrary, in his messages to Job God made it clear that He is in immediate control of His complete creation and all of its creatures (Job 38–41). To the same point the apostle Paul wrote that "in him [Christ] all things hold together" (Col. 1:17). Similarly, the writer of the epistle to the Hebrews stated that God's Son is "sustaining all things by his powerful Word" (Heb. 1:3). The apostle John undoubtedly had the work of sustaining creation in mind when he wrote concerning the Word of God, "In him was life, and that life was the light of men" (John 1:4). Robertson correctly concluded, "The permanence of the universe rests, then, on Christ far more than on gravity. It is a Christo-centric universe. . . . Christ is the controlling and unifying force in nature."[12]

SUMMARY

The biblical truth that Jesus Christ existed prior to His incarnation as the infant Jesus is stated in a number of Scriptures (John 1:14–15, 18, 30; 3:13; 6:62; Phil. 2:5–6). Jesus Himself asked God the Father to "glorify me in your presence with the glory I had with you before the world began" (John 17:5). Only the apostle John, however, identified the preincarnate Christ as the eternal Word who subsists eternally in intimate relationship with God and is identified as God. This introduced the doctrine of the one God of the Bible who subsists as a Trinity of persons. And this, in turn, as well as the apostle John's revelation of the eternal Word's participation in the creation of all things, led to a discussion of the relationship of the three persons of the triune Godhead—God the Father, God the Son (or Word), and God the Holy Spirit—in all the work of God, including the work of creation of all things and the subsequent sustaining of all things.

Two

THE PREINCARNATE MINISTRY
OF THE WORD OF GOD

———◦◎◦———

THE PREINCARNATE MINISTRY of the Lord Jesus Christ as the eternal Word of God began with His participation in the cosmic creative activity of the triune Godhead, discussed in the preceding chapter (Gen. 1:1–2:3; John 1:3; Col. 1:16). His ministry continues in His involvement in sustaining creation in its orderliness and predictability, which people can observe and describe (Col. 1:17). Until the moment of His incarnation as the baby in Bethlehem, however, was His preincarnate ministry limited to these two activities? His very designation as the Word implies otherwise because it suggests visible expression and manifestation and audible communication and revelation. His identity as the Word means that to become incarnate He had to be a member of the Godhead. It also means that He is the member of the Godhead manifested visibly and communicating audibly in the Old Testament. Some evidence supporting this conclusion is definite, while other evidence is more tenuous.

THE PREINCARNATE MINISTRY
OF THE WORD AS THE ANGEL OF THE LORD

One line of evidence for the preincarnate ministry of the Word of God is the ministry of the Angel of the Lord in the Old Testament. The Hebrew word translated "angel," as well as its Greek equivalent, means a person sent as a deputy or representative and a messenger. In fact, the English word *angel* is in effect a transliteration of the Greek word *angelos*. God used members of His angelic hosts as His representatives and messengers, for example, Gabriel (Dan. 8:15–26; 9:11–27; Luke 1:19–20, 26–37), other unnamed angels, such as the two at Jesus' tomb (24:4–7), and the two at Christ's ascension (Acts 1:10–11). The Angel of the Lord who ministered in the Old Testament, however, is a unique representative and messenger of God, as we will discuss. He is in a class by Himself.

This fact is demonstrated by an examination of the recorded appearances of the Angel of the Lord in the Old Testament. The first was to Hagar, the Egyptian servant of Sarai. Sarai gave her to Abram, Sarai's husband, as a concubine when Sarai was infertile (Gen. 16:1–3). When Hagar conceived, she despised her mistress, who dealt with her harshly. As a result Hagar fled from the household (16:4–6). As Moses recorded, "The angel of the LORD found Hagar near a spring in the desert" (16:7). The Angel instructed her to return to Sarai and submit to her. He explained that she would bear a son whom she should call Ishmael and from whom would come many descendants (16:9–12). Hagar gave this name to the One who appeared to her: "You are the God who sees me" (16:13). Some say her identifying this person as God was an error. But note that Moses, the author of Genesis, writing under inspiration of the Holy Spirit, wrote, "She gave this name to the LORD who spoke to her" (16:13).

This Hebrew word for "LORD" is translated in the King James Version and American Standard Version as *Jehovah*, an effort at transliterating the Hebrew word *YHWH*, a four-letter word called the tetragrammaton. A better transliteration is *Yahweh*. When the Jews came to the word *Yahweh* in reading the Old Testament, they refused to pronounce it. This was out of worshipful respect for God and to insure against their blaspheming "the name of the LORD" (Lev. 24:16), a sin punishable by death. Instead they would say either *'Adōnāy* ("Lord") or *'Elōhîm* ("God"), whichever was appropriate in the context. As the Jewish scribes produced their scrolls, they added vowels to the consonants of the Hebrew word for Lord. These vowels are reflected in the English name Jehovah. The word *Yahweh* more accurately reflects the Hebrew consonants.

Further evidence of the careful use of the name Yahweh (LORD) is the statement by God recorded in Isaiah 42:8: "I am the LORD; that is my name! I will not give my glory to another or my praise to idols" (see 43:3, 15). In light of this, for Hagar to identify one of God's angelic hosts, a created spirit being, as Yahweh may seem at first glance to be a mistake. Yet this in fact indicates that the Angel of the Lord is the same as Yahweh.

The facts found in the incident of the Angel of the Lord's appearance to Hagar are repeated in many of His other appearances. It is verified, for example, by His appearance to Abraham (whose name was changed from Abram in Gen. 17:5) when he was about to sacrifice his only heir and son Isaac as a sacrifice to God, as God had commanded (22:1–10). As Abraham stood with the knife in his hand poised above Isaac on the altar, the Angel of the Lord called to Abraham to stay his hand (22:11–12) and provided a substitute sacrifice of a ram caught in a thicket (22:13). Abraham considered the Angel of the Lord who spoke to him to be the Lord Himself, for he "called that place, 'The LORD Will Provide'" (22:14). Also he wrote that the subsequent covenantal promise spoken by the Angel of the Lord was a declaration of the Lord Himself (22:15–18).

Moses knew that the Angel who spoke to Hagar was God Himself, as he wrote in Genesis 16:13, because of his own personal experience at the burning bush, recorded in Exodus 3. "There the angel of the LORD appeared to him in flames of fire from within a bush" (3:2). The account continues, however, "When the LORD [no longer the Angel of the LORD] saw that he had gone over to look, God called to him from within the bush" (3:4) and instructed Moses to remove his sandals because "the place where you are standing is holy ground" (3:5). God then identified Himself as "the God of your father, the God of Abraham, the God of Isaac and the God of Jacob" (3:6). Later God identified Himself as "I AM WHO I AM," and He instructed Moses to tell the Jews in Egypt, "I AM has sent me to you" (3:14). The name I AM is linguistically related to Yahweh.

During the theocracy, when God ruled His people Israel and delivered them from their enemies and oppressors through sovereignly chosen judges (Judg. 2:16–19), the Angel of the Lord appeared at least twice to judges in calling them to their ministries. One occasion was an appearance to Gideon while he was threshing wheat secretly "in a winepress to keep it from the Midianites" (6:11). After first calling this person "the angel of the Lord" (6:11–12), the author of Judges (who was Samuel, according to the Jewish Talmud) called him "the Lord" (6:14, 16–17, 23, 25), as did Gideon (6:15).

Evidently equating the Angel of the Lord with the Lord Himself, Gideon requested permission to bring an "offering and set it before you" (6:18). When Gideon returned with a young goat and unleavened bread, the Angel told him how to prepare it as an offering on a rock. Then the Angel touched the offering with a staff, and it was consumed with fire from the rock and the Angel disappeared (6:19–21). Realizing he had truly seen and talked with the Angel of the Lord, Gideon was afraid he would die (6:22). In response to the Lord's assurance of peace, Gideon "built an altar there to the Lord there and called it 'The Lord is Peace'" (6:24).

In preparation for the birth and ministry of Samson, the Angel of the Lord next appeared to the infertile wife of Manoah, announcing to her that she would conceive and give birth to a son who "is to be a Nazirite, set apart to God from birth" (13:5). When the woman told her husband, Manoah prayed for the Angel's return to give them further instructions, a request God granted (13:8–14). When Manoah prepared a burnt offering to the Lord in response to the Angel's suggestion, the Angel ascended into heaven in the flame of the sacrifice on the altar (13:19–21). "We are doomed to die!" Manoah told his wife; "We have seen God" (13:22). Being more theologically perceptive, Manoah's wife responded, "If the Lord had meant to kill us, he would not have accepted a burnt offering and grain offering from our hands, nor shown us all these things or now told us this" (13:23).

The significant thing about the appearances of the Angel of the Lord to both Gideon and Manoah and his wife, in addition to his identity as the Lord given by both Gideon and Samson's parents, is his acceptance of their worship in the form of sacrificial offering. The created angels of God explicitly refuse to accept worship, saying to those who would do so, "Do not do it! . . . Worship God!" (Rev. 19:10; 22:8). The acceptance of worship by the Angel of the Lord is further evidence that He is the Lord Himself, the preincarnate Word of God.

The Angel of the Lord is mentioned in a number of other incidents in the Old Testament. One is the appearance of the Angel of the Lord to Balaam's donkey (Num. 22:22–27) and then to Balaam himself (22:31–35). In this incident the only possible basis for such an identification is relating the Angel of the Lord's declaration to Balaam, "speak only what I tell you" (22:35), with Balaam's statement to Balak, "I must speak only what God puts in my mouth" (22:38). Further possible but unclear evidence can be found in Moses' declarations, "Then the LORD opened the donkey's mouth" (22:28) and "Then the LORD opened Balaam's eyes" (22:31).

Still other incidents are the Angel of the Lord's appearance and message "to all the Israelites" (Judg. 2:1–5), His appearance to Elijah when he fled into the wilderness from Jezebel (1 Kings 19:5–7), His directing Elijah to confront Ahaziah's messengers (2 Kings 1:3) and Ahaziah (1:15), His judgment on the camp of Assyrian soldiers in siege around Jerusalem (19:35) in answer to King Hezekiah's prayer (19:15–19), His appearance to King David (1 Chron. 21:16) and his message to the prophet Gad (21:18) when God judged Israel for David's numbering of the people.

The Angel of the Lord is mentioned frequently in the visions Zechariah recorded in his prophetic book. For example, the Angel of the Lord is the man "riding a red horse . . . standing among the myrtle trees in a ravine" (Zech. 1:8), as verses 11 and 12 make clear. In the vision of chapter 3, Joshua, the high priest of Israel, was seen "standing before the angel of the LORD, and Satan standing at his right side to accuse him" (3:1). Zechariah then identified the Angel of the Lord as "the LORD," whom he quoted as saying to Satan, "The LORD [referring to God the Father] rebuke you, Satan!" (3:2). Joshua's filthy clothes and turban were changed "while the angel of the LORD stood by" (3:5), and then "the angel of the LORD gave this charge to Joshua" (3:6).

This review of the preincarnate ministry of the Word of God as the Angel of the Lord brings several observations to mind. Of first importance is the fact that His ministry was primarily to leaders of God's chosen people Israel—Abraham, Moses, Gideon, the parents of Samson, David, Elijah, and Zechariah. These appearances also involved the support and protection of Israel, illustrated by His appearance to Balaam and his donkey and his judgment of death on the Assyrian army. Even His judgment of death on Israel for David's prideful numbering of the people ultimately benefited both the king and the nation.

At the same time it is interesting, perhaps even significant, that the ministry of the Angel of the Lord in his first two appearances was "on behalf of a friendless and comfortless person who is not even included in major features of the Abrahamic covenant,"[1] namely, Hagar. This certainly demonstrates God's concern for all downtrodden, needy, oppressed, and poor human beings regardless of race, and reveals His infinite grace, mercy, and comfort. These divine attributes also are displayed in the Angel of the Lord's provision of a substitute sacrifice for Isaac and His provision of food, encouragement, and guidance to distraught and fearful Elijah.

It is important to point out that the Angel of the Lord's defense of Joshua the high priest against the attack of Satan in Zechariah's vision prophetically illustrates the present ministry of the glorified Lord Jesus Christ as "the one who speaks to the Father in our defense" (1 John 2:1) whenever believers sin. Similarly, the Angel of the Lord's provision of a substitute sacrifice for Isaac prophetically illustrates the sacrifice of the incarnate Christ, God's "one and only Son" (John 3:16, 18) as our Substitute, "the righteous for the unrighteous" (1 Pet. 3:18; see Heb. 9:26, 28).

THE PREINCARNATE MINISTRY OF THE WORD AS THE ANGEL OF GOD

Related to the preincarnate ministry of the Word of God as the Angel of the Lord are a few incidents in which He is called the Angel of God. The first of these is another appearance and ministry of comfort, encouragement, and revelation to Hagar (Gen. 21:14–21). For the second time Sarah demanded that Abraham send Hagar away, this time because Ishmael mocked Sarah and Isaac (21:9–10). The bread and water Abraham gave Hagar were soon exhausted in the wilderness, and Hagar left her son under a bush to die while she went some distance away so she would not witness his death (21:14–16).

The Angel of God appeared to Hagar and told her God was aware of her plight (21:17–18). "Then God opened her eyes and she saw a well of water" (21:19), providing life-giving refreshment. Although the conclusion is not irrefutable, the Angel of God here seems to be equated with God. The account adds that "God was with the boy as he grew up" (21:20).

The identity of the Angel of God with God is clearer in the account of His appearance to Jacob while he was with Laban in Haran (31:11). The angel of God told Jacob, "I am the God of Bethel, where you anointed a pillar and where you made a vow to me" (31:13). In that previous dream on the way to Haran the Lord had spoken to Jacob and said, "I am the LORD, the God of your father Abraham and the God of Isaac" (28:13). When Jacob awoke from his dream, he said, "Surely the LORD is in this place" (28:16), and "This is none other than the house of God" (28:17). In the morning he set up a stone as a pillar and consecrated it with oil and called the place Bethel (21:19), which means "House of God."

The Angel of God is mentioned again in the account of the Israelites' departure from Egypt under Moses' human leadership. When the Israelites were pinned against the Red Sea with the Egyptian army in pursuit, "Then the angel of God, who had been traveling in front of Israel's army, withdrew and went behind them. The pillar of cloud also moved from in front and stood behind them" (Exod. 14:19). Here the pillar of cloud is identified with the Angel of God, but previously we read, "By day the LORD went ahead of them in a pillar of cloud to guide them on their way and by night in a pillar of fire to give them light" (13:21). Thus the Angel of God seems to be identified with the Lord.

THE PREINCARNATE MINISTRY OF THE WORD IN OTHER OLD TESTAMENT THEOPHANIES

These appearances of the preincarnate Word of God as the Angel of the Lord and the Angel of God are called theophanies ("appearances of God"), since such appearances are by a member of the triune Godhead. Other appearances of God also are recorded in the Old Testament, which are undoubtedly a part of the preincarnate ministry of the Word of God. In fact, since the eternal Word is the member of the Godhead who manifests and reveals God visibly and audibly, as we have seen, all appearances of God in the Old Testament are part of His preincarnate ministry. What is often difficult to settle is whether a particular appearance is that of God or of a member of His angelic host.

One such case is the record of Joshua's experience after crossing the Jordan River (Josh. 3) and the circumcision of all the males of Israel who had been born in the wilderness (5:2–9). As "Joshua was near Jericho, he looked up and saw a man standing in front of him with a drawn sword in his hand" (5:13). In response to Joshua's question, "Are you for us or for our enemies?" (5:13), the man replied, "Neither . . . but as commander of the army of the LORD I have now come" (5:14). Joshua apparently concluded that this was an appearance of the Lord, because he "fell facedown to the ground in reverence" (5:14). This act of homage was accepted by the man, which was something a mere angel would not be willing to do (Rev. 19:10; 22:8–9). In fact, after commanding Joshua, "Take off your sandals, for the place where you are standing is holy" (Josh. 5:15), the "commander of the LORD's army," now identified as the Lord, gave Joshua directions for the conquest of Jericho.

Another example is the coming of the three men to Abraham in Mamre (Gen. 18:2). Here Moses settled the issue, however, by introducing the incident with the statement, "The LORD appeared to Abraham" (18:1). Although the visitors are called men three times (18:2, 16, 22), one is also identified as "the LORD" (18:10, 13–14, 17, 20, 22, 26–33). After God revealed to Abraham his intentions for Sodom and Gomorrah (18:20–21), "the men turned away and went toward Sodom" (18:22). Apparently only two of the men departed, because "Abraham remained standing before the LORD" (18:22).

A third instance is Jacob's experience the night before he met his brother Esau and was reconciled with him. Jacob was alone, having sent his family and all his possessions across the river Jabbok, "and a man wrestled with him till daybreak" (32:24). The man wrenched Jacob's hip in an effort to overpower him, but Jacob refused to let him go "unless you bless me" (32:26). He renamed Jacob Israel, "because you have struggled with God and with men and have overcome" (32:28), and He "blessed him there" (32:29). "So Jacob called the place Peniel, saying, 'I saw God face to face, and yet my life was spared'" (32:30).

Concerning this incident the prophet Hosea wrote, "As a man he struggled with God. He struggled with the angel and overcame him; he wept and begged for his favor" (Hos. 12:3–4). Then Hosea wrote of Jacob's earlier encounter with God: "He found him at Bethel and talked with him there—the LORD God Almighty, the LORD is his name of renown!" (12:4–5). This inspired commentary confirms the fact that the man with whom Jacob wrestled was the preincarnate Word of God in a theophany.

Still other possible theophanies of the eternal Word of God in the Old Testament include the man who joined Shadrach, Meshach, and Abednego in Nebuchadnezzar's fiery furnace. Nebuchadnezzar said, "Look! I see four men walking around in the fire, unbound and unharmed, and the fourth looks like a son of the gods" (Dan. 3:25). Later he said, "Praise be to the God of Shadrach, Meshach, and Abednego, who has sent his angel and rescued his servants!" (3:28). Daniel had a similar experience when he was thrown into the lions' den (6:16–17). The next morning when King Darius saw Daniel unharmed (16:19–21), the prophet told Darius, "My God sent his angel, and shut the mouths of the lions" (6:22). The conclusion that these incidents are theophanies of the preincarnate Word of God as the Angel of the Lord is appropriate, but not absolutely certain.

Bible students are divided on whether the "man dressed in linen" (10:5) who appeared to Daniel by the Tigris River was a theophany of the preincarnate Word of God as the Angel of the Lord, or whether he was a member of God's angelic host. In support of His identity as the Angel of the Lord is His glorious description (10:6) and His extensive revelation to Daniel of Israel's history from that time forward to the completion of God's program for His chosen people (10:12–12:13). Such a description and such a revelation are appropriate as part of the ministry of the eternal Word of God. (Bible students who conclude this is a member of God's angelic host do so because he was delayed in responding to Daniel's prayers by "the prince of the Persian kingdom" until "Michael, one of the chief princes, came to help me" [10:12–13]. They say no prince could delay the Son of God, but the prince of Persia could delay an angel.)

Although the preincarnate ministry of Jesus Christ as the eternal Word of God began with creation (John 1:3), much of it was directed to God's chosen people Israel (1 Cor. 10:1–4). As already noted, the pillar of cloud and fire that led and protected the Israelites out of Egypt and through the wilderness to Canaan was a preincarnate theophany of the eternal Word of God. In the wilderness the Lord provided manna (Exod. 16:4–5, 35; Josh. 5:12) and quail (Num. 11:31–32) as food for Israel. The Lord also punished Israel when they turned away from Him, but He delivered them from their enemies when they repented and returned to Him (Pss. 105; 106). This seems to be confirmed by Isaiah in his review of God's care of Israel: "In all their distress he too was distressed, and the angel of his presence saved them" (Isa. 63:9). It is also likely that the visible manifestation of the glory of God to Moses, Aaron, Nadab and Abihu, and the seventy elders of Israel (Exod. 24:9–11) and to the people of Israel (24:16–17), to Moses by himself (33:21–23), and to the prophet Ezekiel (Ezek. 1:26–28) were theophanies of the Word of God. In fact, "it is safe to assume that every visible manifestation of God in bodily form in the Old Testament is to be identified with the Lord Jesus Christ"[2] in His preincarnate role as the eternal Word of God.

The emphasis in this chapter on the eternal Word of God ministering in the Old Testament as the Angel of the Lord, the Angel of God, and in other theophanies is not intended to minimize the importance and role of either God the Father or God the Holy Spirit. It simply presents the evidence that the eternal Word of God as a member of the triune Godhead had an active ministry in Old Testament times before His incarnation as the Lord Jesus Christ. In addition, it recognizes the truth of Scripture that God the Father is "invisible" (John 1:18; 6:46; 1 Tim. 1:17; Col. 1:15; 6:15–16; Heb. 11:27; 1 John 4:12) and that God the Holy Spirit also is invisible. The member of the Trinity called "the Word" is the One who manifests and reveals God in incarnate form as Jesus Christ and in preincarnate form as the Angel of the Lord and in other theophanies.

Three

THE OLD TESTAMENT ANTICIPATION OF THE INCARNATION OF THE WORD OF GOD

FTER THE APOSTLE John introduced the eternal Word, who is associated with God as a member of the triune Godhead and was involved in God's work of creation (John 1:1–3), he revealed that "the Word became flesh and made his dwelling among us . . . the One and Only Son, who came from the Father" (1:14). This incarnation of the Word (the Son) as Jesus Christ, the One who has made known the invisible God (1:17–18), suggests that a divine master plan was being carried out. Recognition of such a plan is consistent with the biblical portrait of God as the all-wise Sovereign (Pss. 103:19; 104:24). The Incarnation was not a spur-of-the-moment decision on God's part.

Scripture elsewhere makes it clear that God has a master plan that stretches from eternity to eternity and embraces all created beings, all created things, and all events. Psalm 33:11 reads, "But the plans of the LORD stand firm forever, the purposes of his heart through all generations." Not only is this plan devised in God's infinite wisdom, but also it is carried out by His infinite, sovereign power. "The LORD does whatever pleases him, in the heavens and on the earth, in the seas and all their depths" (135:6). The prophet Isaiah asked, "For the LORD Almighty has purposed, and who can thwart him? His hand is stretched out, and who can turn it back?" (Isa. 14:27; see 46:8–11). King Nebuchadnezzar of

Babylon learned concerning "the Most High . . . who lives forever" that "His dominion is an eternal dominion; his kingdom endures from generation to generation. All the peoples of the earth are regarded as nothing. He does as he pleases with the powers of heaven and the peoples of the earth. No one can hold back his hand or say to him, 'What have you done?'" (Dan. 4:34–35). When Nebuchadnezzar acknowledged God's sovereign control of His universe, he said, "my sanity was restored" (4:34, 36).

The crux of this eternal master plan of God is the redemptive death of Jesus Christ, His incarnate Son (the Word) as a sacrifice for sin to provide salvation and eternal life to all who believe. As the apostle Peter explained to the Jews on the Day of Pentecost, "Jesus of Nazareth . . . was handed over to you by God's set purpose and foreknowledge; and you, with the help of wicked men, put him to death by nailing him to the cross" (Acts 2:22–23). To provide a perfect sacrifice for a redemptive death required the Incarnation, as Peter told his readers: "He was chosen before the creation of the world, but was revealed in these last times for your sake" (1 Pet. 1:20). Similarly, the author of the epistle to the Hebrews wrote, "Therefore, when Christ came into the world, he said . . . 'a body you prepared for me'. . . . Then I said, 'Here I am . . . I have come to do your will, O God'" (Heb. 10:5, 7). The author concluded that "we have been made holy through the sacrifice of the body of Jesus Christ once for all" (10:10).

One part of this master plan difficult to understand is how it can include the eternal choice by God of everyone who will believe in Jesus' sacrificial death while at the same time maintaining that their faith in Jesus' death is their free choice. This is true also of those who refuse to accept the offer of salvation. In fact, this conundrum between God's eternal plan and human will involves all events. Ultimately the answer rests in the mystery of God's omniscience and His sovereignty, but the Bible teaches both the certain execution of God's plan and free will in human choices. For example, the Roman soldiers who crucified Jesus freely chose to divide Jesus' clothing among them and cast lots for his seamless undergarment (John 19:23–24), but their actions had been prophesied in Psalm 22:18.

Contributing to the human choice of salvation is the convicting ministry of God the Holy Spirit (John 16:7–11) and His efficacious calling (Rom. 8:29–30). Such a choice is part of God's master plan. The apostle

Paul told the Ephesians that God "chose us in him before the creation of the world" and "he predestined us to be adopted as his sons through Jesus Christ, in accordance with his pleasure and will" (Eph. 1:4–5). He added, "In him we were also chosen, having been predestined according to the plan of him who works out everything in conformity with the purpose of his will" (1:11). Paul also told the Thessalonians that "from the beginning God chose you to be saved through the sanctifying work of the Spirit and through belief in the truth" (2 Thess. 2:13), and he told Timothy that God "has saved us and called us to a holy life—not because of anything we have done but because of his own purpose and grace" (2 Tim. 1:9).

The goal of this eternal master plan of God is fourfold. The first objective is the exaltation and glorification of Christ, the eternal Word, who willingly humbled himself to become incarnate and to suffer death as a sacrifice for sin in the plan of God (Phil. 2:5–11; see 1 Cor. 15:25–26; Rev. 19:16). A second objective is "that now, through the church, the manifold wisdom of God should be made known to the rulers and authorities in the heavenly realms, according to his eternal purpose which he accomplished in Christ Jesus our Lord" (Eph. 3:10–11). Ultimately this is to be "for the praise of his glory" (1:12, 14) and "to the praise of his glorious grace" (1:6) "so that God may be all in all" (1 Cor. 15:28). A third objective is to bring "many sons to glory" (Heb. 2:10–13)—believers who are "conformed to the likeness of his Son, that he might be the firstborn among many brothers" (Rom. 8:29). A fourth objective is the final defeat and judgment of Satan and all his followers, both angelic and human (Rev. 20:10–15; see Heb. 2:14) and the removal of physical death (1 Cor. 15:25–26).

In view of the fact that the preincarnate Word was ministering to God's chosen people Israel in theanthropic (i.e., deity in human form) appearances during Old Testament times, and since God's eternal plan for His incarnation and sacrificial death was already set, it is not surprising that revelation concerning the incarnation and sacrifice of the Word was presented in what is called prophecy—disclosure in advance of something that will happen. Such prophecy concerning the Incarnation and ministry of God's promised Messiah, our Lord Jesus Christ, is not the total content of Old Testament prophecy, but it is a significant part of it. Since in all its details it is part of God's eternal plan and since God has infinite ability to carry out His plan, why not reveal it in advance as encouragement or warning to God's people? As the Angel of the Lord in theanthropic appearance said to Abraham before the impending destruction of Sodom and Gomorrah, "Shall I hide from Abraham what I am about to do?" (Gen. 18:17).

OLD TESTAMENT ANTICIPATION IN PROPHECY

God's promise to His chosen people Israel of a Messiah permeates the Old Testament and includes prophecies of the Incarnation and ministry of a unique person, even one divine. Some of the prophecies are vague and veiled, but others are quite clear and specific in details. These prophecies are found throughout the Old Testament from the opening chapters of Genesis to the book of the prophet Malachi.

Genesis 3:15. The first Old Testament prophecy concerning the Incarnation and ministry of a Deliverer was part of God's sentence of judgment on the serpent for having led Adam and Eve into sin. God said, "I will put enmity between you and the woman, and between your offspring and hers; he will crush your head, and you will strike his heel." The vagueness of this prophecy is seen in the fact that many commentators suggest that Eve's exclamation at the birth of Cain—"With the help of the LORD I have brought forth a man" (4:1)—is an expression of her hope that he would be the promised offspring to bruise the serpent's head. Ironically, the first murderer, Cain, proved to be the offspring of the serpent instead! As the outworking of God's plan is recorded in Scripture, the offspring of the woman is Jesus Christ, whose heel was bruised in His arrest, trial, and crucifixion. In turn His bruising of the serpent's (i.e., Satan's, Rev. 12:9; 20:2) head began with His resurrection and ascension to heaven and will be consummated when Satan is bound and thrown "into the Abyss" for the millennium (20:2–3) and then thrown "into the lake of burning sulphur, where the beast and the false prophet had been thrown" (20:10; see 19:20) and where the unregenerate human host will be consigned immediately after the Great White Throne judgment (20:11–15).

Genesis 12:3; 18:18; 22:18. These prophetic promises to Abram (later Abraham), beginning with the Lord's call to him to leave his home country and his family to go to a land that God would show him, include the promise that all peoples on earth will be blessed through you." The third occurrence of this promise (22:18) followed Abraham's willingness to obey God in offering Isaac, his only son, as a sacrifice to Him. The author of the epistle to the Hebrews explains that "Abraham reasoned that God could raise the dead" (11:19), but God spared Abraham from the actual sacrifice, providing a ram caught in a thicket by its horns as a substitute (Gen. 22:12–13). For his obedience by faith God promised Abraham that "through your offspring all nations on earth will be blessed" (22:18).

Once again the prophetic promise as originally stated to Abraham seems vague, but the apostle Peter related it to the resurrected Christ (Acts 3:25). Then the apostle Paul clarified that the promise is specifically fulfilled in the Lord Jesus Christ: "The promises were spoken to Abraham and to his seed. The Scripture does not say 'and to seeds,' meaning many people, but 'and to your seed,' meaning one person, who is Christ" (Gal. 3:16). Earlier in that chapter Paul had pointed out that "the Scripture foresaw that God would justify the Gentiles by faith, and announced the gospel in advance to Abraham: 'All nations will be blessed through you'" (3:8).

Genesis 49:8–12. All the prophetic deathbed blessings of Jacob to his twelve sons are important. The most significant, however, is the blessing to Judah, which is identified as the regal tribe—"your brothers will praise you." Judah is called "a lion's cub" and is described as powerful and awesome, like a lion or lioness. He will be victorious over his enemies and "your brothers will praise you." These details of the blessing were fulfilled by David, who was of the tribe of Judah, and by Solomon, his son.

The remainder of Jacob's blessing of Judah had its beginning in David but continues in force today, though it is not completely fulfilled. It reads, "The scepter will not depart from Judah, nor the ruler's staff from between his feet, until he comes to whom it belongs and the obedience of nations is his" (49:10). The angel Gabriel in his message to the Virgin Mary concerning the birth of her Holy-Spirit-conceived son tied this prophecy to the Lord Jesus Christ, saying, "The Lord God will give him the throne of his father David, and he will reign over the house of Jacob forever; his kingdom will never end" (Luke 1:32b–33; see Ps. 2:7–9; Isa. 9:6–7).

Even though the Lord Jesus presented Himself in His ministry to the

Jewish people as the Messiah, the King of the Jews, and was crucified under that caption (John 19:19–22; see Matt. 27:37; Mark 15:26; Luke 23:38), it is obvious that these prophecies were not fulfilled at His first coming. Their fulfillment awaits His return to earth at His second coming in triumph and glory as "King of kings and Lord of lords" (Rev. 19:16) to establish His worldwide reign of righteousness and peace for a thousand years (20:4–6). The closing verses of Jacob's prophetic blessing on Judah (Gen. 49:11–12) poetically picture the abundance and prosperity that will characterize that millennial kingdom reign.

Deuteronomy 18:15–19. God had originally spoken directly to the assembly of Israel at Sinai out of the fire (Deut. 5:4). Out of fear, however, the elders of Israel asked Moses to be a mediator between God and them, receiving the message from God and delivering it to the people (see 18:16). This marked the beginning of the office of prophet, a person who receives God's message and delivers it to the people. Moses was the first, and in many respects, the preeminent prophet. Now in these verses, after forbidding Israel to use sorcery and divination as the heathen do, God promised to "raise up for them a prophet like you from among their brothers" (18:18; see v. 15).

Even though in both verses (18:15, 18) the singular—"a prophet"—is used, most commentators agree that this promise of God refers first to the procession of prophets who proclaimed His messages to Israel during the years after Moses, many of whom wrote the Old Testament prophetic books. In the general sense of being God's chosen instrument to deliver His message to the people, each of the prophets was like Moses. At the same time, however, Scripture makes it clear that Moses stood alone because "no prophet has risen in Israel like Moses, whom the LORD knew face to face" (34:10).

As a result, therefore, most Bible scholars recognize that the promise of a prophet like Moses ultimately is fulfilled in our Lord Jesus Christ. Even the people of Israel anticipated one who would fulfill this promise of a prophet like Moses in a final and ultimate sense, and they related His appearance to the coming of Elijah and the hope for Messiah. This is seen in the questions of the priests and Levites from the Jews of Jerusalem to John the Baptist, such as, "Are you the Prophet?" (John 1:21; see vv. 19–24).

Likewise, after He fed the five thousand, the people "began to say, 'Surely this is the Prophet who is come into the world'" (6:14). In his message to the people after the healing of the lame man in the temple gate Peter specifically identified Jesus as the fulfillment of this promise to Moses (Acts 3:17–23) and Stephen did the same (7:37).

1 Samuel 2:35. In conjunction with His judgment on Hophni and Phinehas, the ungodly sons of Eli the priest, God said, "I will raise up for myself a faithful priest, who will do according to what is in my heart and mind. I will firmly establish his house, and he will minister before my anointed one always." The short-range fulfillment of this prophecy came when King Solomon removed Abiathar, a descendant of Aaron's son Ithamar, as priest (1 Kings 2:26–27), replacing him with Zadok, a descendant of Aaron's son Eleazar. Even though Zadok's descendants proved unfaithful to God from time to time, they continued as high priests until service in the temple ended with its destruction by the Romans in A.D. 70 (see Mal. 2:1–9). In conjunction with the return of Christ to earth and the establishment of His millennial kingdom, however, the priesthood will be established with the descendants of Levi (3:3–4), and the descendants of Zadok will offer sacrifices (Ezek. 44:17–19). In the final sense the Lord Jesus Christ, "a priest forever, in the order of Melchizedek" (Ps. 110:4; see Heb. 4:14–5:7; 7:11–8:2)—is the fulfillment of God's promise of a "faithful priest, who will do according to what is in my [God's] heart and mind" (1 Sam. 2:35).

2 Samuel 7:11–13, 16 (see 1 Chron. 17:10b–11, 12b–14). Although not mentioned as such in these passages, these promises from God to David and his offspring are called "an everlasting covenant" by David (2 Sam. 23:5) as well as by others (Pss. 89:3, 28, 34, 39; 132:11–12). The immediate fulfillment was carried out by Solomon, David's son, who built the temple as the house of God in Jerusalem (1 Kings 6:1–38; 7:13–8:66). God's promise that "your house and your kingdom will endure forever before me; your throne will be established forever" (2 Sam. 7:16), however, extends far beyond Solomon. Ultimately it is fulfilled in our Lord Jesus Christ.

Even though the exercise of regal authority on the throne of David in Jerusalem has been interrupted because of sin, as God warned (7:14), prophets of Israel recognized an eschatological, messianic restoration and fulfillment of God's promise. Concerning the child to be born and the son given who will rule in the future, Isaiah prophesied, "He will reign on David's throne and over his kingdom, establishing and upholding it with justice and righteousness from that time on and forever," declaring, "The zeal of the LORD Almighty will accomplish this" (Isa. 9:7). Likewise Jeremiah prophesied, "'The days are coming,' declares the LORD, 'when I will raise up to David a righteous Branch, a King who will reign wisely and do what is just and right in the land. In his days Judah will be saved and Israel will live in safety. This is the name by which he will be called: The LORD Our Righteousness'" (Jer. 23:5–6; see 33:14–16). Amos also prophesied about a future day when the Lord "will restore David's fallen tent" (Amos 9:11), and Micah predicted that out of Bethlehem Ephrathah "will come for me one who will be ruler over Israel, whose origins are from of old, from ancient times" (Mic. 5:2). All these prophecies will be fulfilled in Jesus Christ, to whom "the Lord God will give . . . the throne of his father David" to "reign over the house of Jacob forever; his kingdom will never end" (Luke 1:32–33). This will be fulfilled when Christ returns to earth and establishes His millennial reign.

Psalm 2:7–9. The Lord's decree, mentioned in verse 7, "refers to the Davidic Covenant [2 Sam. 7:14a] in which God declared that He would be Father to the king, and the king would be His son."[1] The statement, "You are my Son; today I have become your Father," was an ancient Near Eastern formula used when kings were enthroned. This applies, as verses 8–9 reveal, to the establishment of Christ's millennial kingdom. The angel Gabriel, however, announced to the Virgin Mary that her son "will be called the Son of the Most High" (Luke 1:32) and "the Son of God" (1:35) and that "the Lord God will give him the throne of his father David, and he will reign over the house of Jacob forever; his kingdom will never end" (1:32–33). Furthermore, when the Holy Spirit descended on Jesus at His baptism "in bodily form like a dove," a "voice came from heaven: 'You are my Son, whom I love; with you I am well pleased'" (Luke 3:22; see Matt. 3:16–17; Mark 1:10–11; John 1:32–34). As a result the statement in Psalm 2:7 does have relevance to Jesus' incarnation and earthly ministry.

Psalm 16:8–10. These verses express David's confident faith in God, especially in God's protection and deliverance from death. God's shield of protection delivered Israel's warrior king in many battles, but finally in old age death overtook him (1 Kings 2:10). In a real sense, therefore, David's expressed hope that God will not "let your Holy One see decay" (Ps. 16:10) transcends his personal experience. The apostle Peter made this clear in his sermon on the Day of Pentecost when he quoted these verses of Psalm 16 and pointed out that David, a prophet, was predicting the resurrection of Jesus Christ from the tomb without His body having experienced decay (Acts 2:25–32). In his sermon at Antioch in Pisidia the apostle Paul also quoted the clause, "You will not let your Holy One see decay," and applied it to Jesus' resurrection (13:35–36). Concerning Psalm 16:10 Allen Ross wrote, "Preservation from the decaying grave is the idea behind both David's and Jesus' experiences, but with David it came through a *deliverance* from death, whereas with Jesus it came through a *resurrection* from death."[2]

Psalm 22:1, 6–8, 12–18. Evangelical Bible students have difficulty deciding when in David's life he experienced the mental and physical affliction and suffering expressed in this psalm, especially in verses 1–18. The majority place it during the time of King Saul's pursuit of David and his men, but the record in 1 Samuel does not reflect such mental, emotional, or physical suffering, nor a sense of being abandoned by God (Ps. 22:1). Others place it during David's flight from Jerusalem across the Jordan River to Mahanaim after his son Absalom's revolt (2 Sam. 15–18). Although this experience has some similarities, Ross rightly concludes, "No known incident in the life of David fits the details of this psalm."[3]

In the New Testament it is evident that Jesus Christ and the Gospel authors recognized and stated connections between this psalm and the crucifixion and death of Jesus. Shortly before Jesus "gave up his spirit" (Matt. 27:50; John 19:30) He "cried out in a loud voice, '*Eloi, Eloi, lama sabachthani?*'—which means, 'My God, my God, why have you forsaken me?'" (Matt. 27:46; Mark 15:34). This is a direct quotation of Psalm 22:1; it is most fitting because at that moment Jesus was bearing the judgment of God for the sin of the world (2 Cor. 5:21; see John 1:29, 35; Rom. 4:25).

Matthew recorded that "the chief priests, the teachers of the law and the elders mocked" Jesus on the cross (Matt. 27:41), taunting him to come down from the cross, and then they would believe. They quoted Psalm 22:8, saying "He trusts in God. Let God rescue him now if he wants him" (Matt. 27:43). The passersby also "hurled insults at him" (Matt. 27:39; Mark 15:19), "the soldiers also came up and mocked him" (Luke 23:36), and even "the robbers [at least one of them] who were crucified with him also heaped insults on him" (Matt. 27:44; Mark 15:32). The other robber, recognizing Jesus' innocence, asked to be remembered when Jesus came into His kingdom, a request Jesus promised to grant (Luke 23:39–43). These passages from the Gospels fulfill Psalm 22:6–8.

Concerning Psalm 22 Ross observed, "The expressions describe an execution, not an illness; yet that execution is more appropriate to Jesus' crucifixion than David's experience. . . . David used many poetic expressions to portray his immense sufferings, but these poetic words became literally true of the suffering of Jesus Christ at his enemies' hands."[4] This is especially true in Psalm 22:12–18, climaxing with the soldiers taking his clothes and "dividing them into four shares, one for each of them" and casting lots for his "undergarment" (tunic), which "was seamless, woven in one piece from top to bottom" (John 19:23; see Matt. 27:35; Mark 15:24; Luke 23:34). The apostle John observed that this "happened that the Scripture might be fulfilled" and quoted Psalm 22:16 (John 19:24).

Psalm 40:6–8. In these verses David, a man after God's own heart (Acts 13:22; see 1 Sam. 13:14), recognized that God desires a committed life of obedient service (Rom. 12:1) more than sacrifices and offerings, and so he dedicated himself to do God's will. Though David failed to fulfill this commitment totally, which is true of each of us as well, it was fulfilled perfectly in the incarnation and ministry of Jesus Christ. Jesus told the Jews, "I do nothing on my own but speak just what the Father has taught me. . . . I always do what pleases him" (John 8:28–29); the author of the epistle to the Hebrews quoted these verses from Psalm 40 as fulfilled "when Christ came into the world" (Heb. 10:5–7). The writer's words, "a body you prepared for me," are quoted from the Septuagint, an ancient Greek translation. These words pertaining to Jesus' body are appropriate to the context as well as to the Incarnation.

Many other statements in the Psalms are quoted in the New Testament as fulfilled in the life and ministry of our Lord (e.g., Pss. 45:6–7 [Heb. 1:8–9]; 68:18 [Eph. 4:8]; 110:1 [Heb. 1:13]). Numerous others are fulfilled by incidents in Jesus' life and ministry without the Gospel writer explicitly saying he was referring to the passages in the Psalms (e.g., [Matt. 26:14–16; Mark 14:10–11, 44; Luke 22:47–48]; 69:21 [Matt. 27:48; Mark 15:36; John 19:29]). These underscore the wealth of Old Testament prophecies that anticipate the incarnation and ministry of Christ.

Isaiah 7:14. This prophecy obviously had an imminent fulfillment because it was announced by Isaiah as a sign from the Lord to King Ahaz, who with false piety refused to "put the Lord to the test" by asking for a sign (7:12–13). To serve as a sign to Ahaz, the young virgin, her marriage, and the birth and naming of her son Immanuel would probably have to have been known to Ahaz. Within approximately three years of Isaiah's giving God's sign, the kingdoms of Syria and Israel in alliance against Judah were conquered and destroyed by Tiglath-Pileser, king of Assyria, in fulfillment of the sign.

Some Bible students believe this prophecy and the sign have only an immediate significance and fulfillment. According to this view, the angel's announcement to Joseph about Mary's conception (Matt. 1:22–23) was merely coincidental. A second view considers the prophecy applicable only to our Lord Jesus Christ, because it is addressed to the "house of David" (Isa. 7:13), not specifically to Ahaz, who was then the Davidic king. This view does not eliminate an immediate significance of the message, because approximately three years afterward the northern kingdom of Israel and Damascus would no longer be formidable foes of Judah. A third position combines these two views, recognizing both an immediate sign to Ahaz and the house of David and an ultimate fulfillment in the conception and birth of our Lord by the Virgin Mary.

Isaiah 9:6–7. This prophecy of Israel's Messiah is at least partially fulfilled with the incarnation of our Lord Jesus Christ in that He is described as a child and as a son. At the same time "he will be called Wonderful Counselor, Mighty God, Everlasting Father, Prince of Peace," titles and qualities that will be displayed in His rulership in peace, justice, and righteousness "on David's throne and over his kingdom . . . from that time on and forever" (9:6–7). The prophecy joins the birth of the Child with the rulership of the King without mentioning the obvious necessary lapse of time between them, that is, between Jesus' first advent and His still future second coming as "King of kings and Lord of lords" (Rev. 19:16). As John Walvoord observes, "In this passage, as in many passages in the Old Testament, the first and second comings of Christ were not distinguished."[5]

Isaiah 11:1–12:6. This extended passage predicts a coming "shoot . . . from the stump of Jesse," a prophecy fulfilled in the incarnation of Christ, who was in the line of descent legally through Joseph (Matt. 1:16) and physically through Mary (Luke 3:31–32). Part of the prophecy was fulfilled in Jesus' first coming because in His life and ministry He did enjoy the presence of the "Spirit of the Lord . . . the Spirit of wisdom and of understanding, the Spirit of counsel and of power, the Spirit of knowledge and of the fear of the LORD" (Isa. 11:2), and he did "delight in the fear of the LORD" (11:3). All this will also characterize our Lord Jesus Christ's second coming and millennial reign over the whole world as described in the rest of the passage. This event is identified as occurring "in that day" when "the Root of Jesse will stand as a banner for the peoples" (11:10; 12:1, 4).

Isaiah 40:3–5. This prophecy is related to Jesus' incarnation because it is identified with the ministry of John the Baptist, His forerunner. Verses 4 and 5 speak of events that will occur as part of Christ's second coming, but its identification with the ministry of John the Baptist shows that the Lord Jesus was presented then as Israel's Messiah and Savior and, had they recognized and received Him as such, the kingdom would have begun. John's message to Israel was, "Repent, for the kingdom of heaven is near"(Matt. 3:2; see Mark 1:4; Luke 1:17; 3:3; John 1:6-8). Matthew then wrote, "This is he who was spoken of through the prophet Isaiah" and he quoted Isaiah 40:3 (Matt. 3:3; see Mark 1:2–3; Luke 3:4–6; John 1:23).

Isaiah 49:1–7. This passage begins a section of Isaiah's prophetic book generally recognized as the prophecy concerning the Servant of the Lord (chaps. 49–57). Isaiah 49 begins with the servant speaking: "Before I was born the LORD called me; from my birth he has made mention of my name. . . . He said to me, 'You are my servant, Israel, in whom I will display my splendor'" (49:1, 3). To this the servant responded that He had accomplished nothing and His labor had been in vain but He would leave His reward with His God (49:4).

Because the Lord addressed His servant as Israel, the Jewish people consider themselves the servant charged with carrying the message of the one true God to everyone. As the passage continues, however, this conclusion cannot be supported. The servant said that the Lord "formed me in the womb to be his servant, to bring Jacob back to him and gather Israel to himself" (49:5), hardly possible if the servant is Israel. Later the servant described Himself as "him who was despised and abhorred by the nation," Israel (49:7). We must remember that the name Israel, meaning "a ruler with God," was given to Jacob when he wrestled with the Angel of the Lord at the Jabbok River the night before he met his brother Esau (Gen. 32:24–28). The name obviously was applied to the descendants of Jacob and to the nation they became, but it is applied here to God's Servant, who is and will be a Ruler with God.

This servant is Jesus Christ, called by the Lord before His birth to be God's Servant. He was indeed "despised and abhorred by the nation," the people of Israel, to the point that they cried to Pilate, "Crucify him!" (Matt. 27:22–23, 25; see Mark 15:12–14; Luke 23:21; John 19:6, 15). In God the Father's conversation with Him, God told Him, "'It is too small a thing for you to be my servant to restore the tribes of Jacob, and bring back those of Israel I have kept. I will also make you a light to the Gentiles, that you may bring my salvation to the ends of the earth'" (Isa. 49:6). This clarifies the identification of the Servant with Christ.

Isaiah 61:1–2. This passage, including the verses that follow in this chapter, are the proclamation of the Servant of the Lord about His ministry. Our Lord Jesus Christ read verse 1 and the first clause of verse 2 when He returned to His hometown of Nazareth and was asked to read the Scripture in the synagogue on the Sabbath (Luke 4:16–19). He deliberately ended his reading with the clause "to proclaim the year of the Lord's favor" in the middle of verse 2, because that ended the description of His ministry in His first coming. The remainder of verse 2 describes His ministry at His return to earth in "vengeance" and triumph. With the audience obviously expecting Him to continue reading the passage, Jesus said to them, "Today this scripture is fulfilled in your hearing" (Luke 4:21).

Jeremiah 23:5–6; 33:15–17. In Isaiah 11:1, 10 the Messiah is called a "shoot . . . from the stump of Jesse," David's father. But in Jeremiah He is called "a righteous Branch . . . from David's line" (33:15) because in the

New Testament He is said to fulfill promises to David (Luke 1:32–33; see 2 Tim. 2:8; Rev. 5:5; 22:18). Although Jesus is David's Branch from His conception, His ministry as such is identified primarily with His return to earth at His second coming and His millennial reign on David's throne. This is substantiated by the references to the Branch in Zechariah 3:8 and 6:12. However, during His ministry in His first coming the people Jesus healed frequently called Him the "Son of David" (Matt. 9:27; 12:23; 15:22; 20:30–31; Mark 10:47–48; Luke 18:38–39). Also, as He rode into Jerusalem on a donkey on the day now called Palm Sunday, His followers then called Him "the Son of David" (Matt. 21:9, 15). That incident is specifically predicted in Zechariah 9:9, where the "Daughter of Zion . . . Jerusalem" is called on to rejoice and shout because "your king comes to you, righteous and having salvation, gentle and riding on a donkey, on a colt, the foal of a donkey." Critics complain that this fulfillment was deliberately arranged by Jesus, which is undoubtedly true (Matt. 21:1–11; Mark 11:1–10; Luke 19:28–40; John 12:12–16); but it was done to confront the Jewish leaders and people one last time with the opportunity to recognize and accept Him as God's promised Messiah.

Zechariah 12:10; 13:7. These two prophecies of Zechariah relate to the incarnation and first-coming ministry of Jesus Christ, specifically His rejection and crucifixion. This is especially true of the call, "'Awake, O sword, against my shepherd, against the man who is close to me!' declares the LORD Almighty, 'Strike the shepherd, and the sheep will be scattered.'" Jesus quoted this latter statement in predicting the scattering of His disciples at His arrest and crucifixion (Matt. 26:31; Mark 14:27). Zechariah 12:10 describes the mourning and sorrow of the people of Israel when the Lord Jesus will return to be their King and they recognize Him as "the one they have pierced."

Once again numerous additional prophecies in the Old Testament prophetic books fulfilled in our Lord Jesus Christ could be mentioned. For example, Micah 5:2 (already mentioned) and Malachi 3:1 ("the messenger of the covenant, whom you desire, will come") relate to His incarnation and first-coming ministry. As Jesus told his disciples when He appeared to them after His resurrection, "Everything must be fulfilled that is written about me in the Law of Moses, the Prophets and the Psalms"

(Luke 24:44). Peter, after healing the lame man at the temple gate called Beautiful, said in his sermon to the people, "this is how God fulfilled what he had foretold through all the prophets, saying that his Christ would suffer. . . . Indeed, all the prophets from Samuel on, as many as have spoken, have foretold these days" (Acts 3:18, 24). The majority of the remaining Old Testament prophecies about the Messiah, however, predict His return to earth at His second coming and describe the establishing of His millennial kingdom and reign (discussed in chaps. 11–13).

OLD TESTAMENT ANTICIPATIONS IN TYPOLOGY

Typology is an aspect of biblical theology that deals with parallels between the Old and New Testaments involving Jesus Christ and His body, the church. The word *type* transliterates the Greek word *typos,* which, with its synonyms, provides the basis for this study. A "type" has been defined, then, as "an event, person, or object which by its very nature and significance prefigures or foreshadows some later event, person, or object."[6] The New Testament provides the basis for this study by identifying certain things as types. For example, the apostle Paul described Adam as "a pattern [*typos,* type] of the one to come [Jesus Christ]" (Rom. 5:14), and he spoke of the experiences of the Israelites in the wilderness "as examples [*typoi*] . . . written down as warnings for us" (1 Cor. 10:11; see v. 6).

The fact that types are identified as such in the New Testament shows that typology is a legitimate part of biblical and theological study. It also demonstrates that types are a part of God's eternal master plan with a definite purpose in His program and revelation in Scripture. They are not simply coincidental similarities between things in the Old Testament and aspects of Jesus' life and ministry that happened to be noticed by Him and the New Testament writers. Types correspond in many respects with Old Testament prophecies and constitute predictions and anticipations of what is to come as God's master plan unfolds. Also, like Old Testament prophecy (Rev. 19:10), types focus in their New Testament antitypes on the person and work of Christ.

In the study of typology two extremes have surfaced. On the one hand some writers tend to see more types in Scripture than can reasonably be justified. They also tend to force a comparison between every detail of the Old Testament type and its antitype. As Wick Broomall notes, "Sober exegesis must prevail over wild fancies. . . . At the other extreme are found those who refuse to see in OT history any typical meaning. The true view is found between these extremes."[7] Some Bible students restrict their identification of types to the things specifically identified as such in the New Testament; however, this seems too restrictive because Paul indicated that Israel's wilderness experiences, without mentioning specifics, "occurred as examples *[typoi]*" (1 Cor 10:6). The following are some of the types recognized by most evangelicals.

Adam (Rom. 5:14; 1 Cor. 15:22, 45–49). The typical relationship between the first man, Adam, and Jesus Christ is not surprising. But the relationship includes both a comparison or parallelism—Adam "was a pattern *[typos]* of the one to come" (Rom. 5:14)—and also contrasting (anti-thetical) connections. This latter aspect is stated in 1 Corinthians 15:22—"For as in Adam all die, so in Christ all will be made alive." The apostle discussed the contrast between Adam and Jesus Christ more fully in 1 Corinthians 15:45–49. Quoting Genesis 2:7, he wrote "So it is written, 'The first man Adam became a living being'; the last Adam, a life-giving spirit. The spiritual did not come first, but the natural, and after that the spiritual. The first man was of the dust of the earth, the second man from heaven. As was the earthly man, so are those who are of the earth; and as is the man from heaven, so also are those who are of heaven. And just as we have borne the likeness of the earthly man, so shall we bear the likeness of the man from heaven." As human beings we cannot avoid bearing the likeness of Adam and the sentence of physical and spiritual death for sin through him, but the choice of spiritual life and eternity with God through faith in Christ's redemptive death is available to every person.

Noah, the Ark, and the Flood. A number of Scriptures present Noah—his preparation of the ark in obedience to God for the deliverance of his family and the animals—as a type of present spiritual experiences and of future judgment. This is done simply by drawing a comparison between Noah and his experience and what it illustrates: "As it was in the days of Noah, so it will be in the coming of the Son of Man" (Matt. 24:37; Luke 17:26). Matthew then described how people were continuing on their daily routines with-

out heeding Noah's message of impending judgment until the Flood suddenly overtook them (Matt. 24:38–39). Luke drew the same comparison
with the rescue of Lot and God's judgment on Sodom and Gomorrah
(17:28–29). The apostle Peter also used the experiences both of Noah and
of Lot as examples of God's ability to rescue the godly from His judgment
on the ungodly (2 Pet. 2:5–9).

The apostle Peter also stated that in the ark "only a few people, eight
in all, were saved through water, and this water symbolizes baptism that
now saves you also—not the removal of dirt from the body but the pledge
of a good conscience toward God. It saves you by the resurrection of Jesus
Christ, who has gone into heaven and is at God's right hand" (1 Pet. 3:20–22).
Some churches teach that Peter's statements that Noah and his family
"were saved through water" and that "this water . . . saves you" mean that
water baptism is necessary for salvation. But, as A.T. Robertson explains,
this "saving" by water is "only symbolic . . . not actual. Baptism, Peter
explains, does not wash away the filth of the flesh either in a literal sense,
as a bath for the body, or in a metaphorical sense of the filth of the soul. . . .
Peter here expressly denies baptismal remission of sin."[8] Roger Raymer
also comments on the significance of water baptism: "Baptism represents
a complete break with one's past life. . . . The act of public baptism would
'save' them [Peter's readers] from the temptation to sacrifice their good
consciences in order to avoid persecution. For a first-century Christian,
baptism meant he was following through on his commitment to Christ,
regardless of the consequences."[9]

Melchizedek. Identified as "king of Salem," Melchizedek was also a
"priest of God Most High" (Gen. 14:18), who blessed Abraham after his
defeat of Kedorlaomer and the rescue of Lot and his possessions (14:19–20),
and to whom Abraham gave "a tenth of everything" (14:20). Melchizedek's
priesthood preceded the Levitical priesthood of Aaron and his descendants in both time and significance. God's Messiah is as "a priest forever,
in the order of Melchizedek" (Ps. 110:4) in the unchanging decree of God.
This is the basis for Melchizedek's serving as a type of Christ both in His
sacrifice of Himself on the cross as God's redemptive and propitiatory
offering for sin, and in His present ministry for believers in the presence
of God (Heb. 2:17; 4:14–5:10; 6:19–10:25).

Isaac. Without specifically being so identified, Isaac serves as a type of Christ because Scripture calls him Abraham's "one and only son" (Heb. 11:17), whom Abraham by faith offered as a sacrifice to God. Although God spared Isaac's life (Gen. 22:10–12), Abraham was committed to the sacrifice, reasoning "that God could raise the dead, and figuratively speaking, he did receive Isaac back from death" (Heb. 11:19). Jesus Christ is God's "one and only Son" (John 1:14; 3:16, 18; 1 John 4:9), whom God "did not spare . . . but gave him up for us all" (Rom. 8:32). As a result the Lord Jesus is typified in a sense by the "ram caught by its horns" that Abraham offered as a sacrifice in Isaac's place (Gen. 22:13), because Jesus is our Substitute who bore the judgment of God for our sins (2 Cor. 5:21; Gal. 3:13). In addition to serving as a type of Christ, Isaac, together with his brother Ishmael as well as their mothers Hagar and Sarah, serve as an allegorical illustration of two covenants—the Mosaic Covenant of law at Mount Sinai and the Abrahamic Covenant of promise fulfilled in Christ (Gal. 4:21–31).

David. Jesus Christ, as already discussed, is David's prophesied Offspring who will occupy his throne and "reign over the house of Jacob forever; his kingdom will never end" (Luke 1:32–33). David also, however, serves as a type of Christ, even though that is not specifically stated in Scripture. First, David illustrates Jesus in that, although he was guilty of grievous sins, God called him "a man after my own heart; he will do everything I want him to do" (Acts 13:22; see 1 Sam. 13:14). God called the Lord Jesus "my Son, whom I love; with him I am well pleased" (Matt. 3:17; see Mark 1:11; Luke 3:22), and Jesus said, "I always do what pleases him" (John 8:29; Rom. 15:3). In addition, when the Pharisees accused Jesus and His disciples of breaking the Sabbath because they plucked and ate some heads of grain when they were hungry, Jesus reminded them of David's action in entering "the house of God" and eating "the consecrated bread" when he was hungry (Matt. 12:3–4; Mark 2:25–26; Luke 6:3–4; see 1 Sam. 21:3–6). Then He said concerning Himself, "I tell you that one [lit., 'something'] greater than the temple is here. . . . For the Son of Man is Lord of the Sabbath" (Matt. 12:6, 8).

Jonah. Jesus Christ personally identified the prophet Jonah and his experience in the large fish as a type of His resurrection. When the Pharisees demanded of Him a miraculous sign to validate His messianic claims, Jesus said they would receive no sign "except the sign of the prophet Jonah. For as Jonah was three days and three nights in the belly of a huge fish, so the Son of Man will be three days and three nights in the heart of the earth" (Matt. 12:39–40; see Luke 11:29–30), thus predicting His resurrection. Explaining that the people of Nineveh repented at Jonah's message, He said, "And now one [lit., 'something'] greater than Jonah is here" (Matt. 12:41; Luke 11:32).

Many other valid types could be mentioned, ones specifically identified in Scripture as well as others that are not. For example, the Lord Jesus compared Himself to the bronze snake Moses lifted up on a pole to provide healing from the deadly venomous snakebites with a glance of faith (Num. 21:8–9). Jesus told Nicodemus, "Just as Moses lifted up the snake in the desert, so the Son of Man must be lifted up [referring to His death on the cross], that everyone who believes in him may have eternal life" (John 3:14–15). Other types include the mercy seat (Rom. 3:25) and the Passover (1 Cor. 5:7).

As mentioned before, Paul identified the experiences of the Israelites in the wilderness "as examples *[typoi]*, to keep us from setting our hearts on evil things as they did" (1 Cor. 10:6; see v. 11). In addition, the earthly tabernacle erected in the wilderness according to the specifications given to Moses corresponds to the heavenly tabernacle into which our Lord Jesus Christ has entered and where He ministers (Heb. 9:1–10:25); the Levitical priesthood is contrasted with Jesus' priesthood after the order of Melchizedek (7:11–28); and the Mosaic Covenant is contrasted with the New Covenant (8:1–13). Hebrews also compares and contrasts Moses, who "was faithful as a servant in all God's house"—with Christ, "who is faithful as a son over God's house" (3:2–6). In fact, in a true sense all those in Hebrews 11 who lived by faith serve as types and examples for believers today.

CONCLUSION

This study of Old Testament anticipations of the incarnation and ministry of our Lord Jesus Christ in His first coming, His present ministry, and His future return and ministry should strengthen our faith in the Lord and encourage us to worship and serve Him more zealously. Without question God is in control of His world and He is working out His master plan according to His schedule. Believers may not know what the future holds from day to day, but they know who holds the future and they can trust Him.

Part 2

THE INCARNATE
SON OF GOD

Four

THE NAMES AND TITLES
OF THE SON OF GOD

———◆———

THE PRECEDING CHAPTERS discussed the Lord Jesus' identity as the eternal Word of God, the second person of the triune Godhead, and His preincarnate ministry as the Angel of the Lord in His various manifestations. A discussion of the primary names and titles given to Him is now appropriate.

THE LORD JESUS CHRIST

The title "the Lord Jesus Christ," the full Christian name of our Lord, bears witness to His deity, His humanity, and His ministry of providing salvation. The Gospels do not record this full title being addressed to Jesus in His earthly ministry.

The first usage of it recorded in Scripture was by Peter when he was explaining his ministry of the gospel to the Gentiles to the believers in Jerusalem (Acts 11:17). The next recorded usage was also by Peter at the council in Jerusalem (15:11; see v. 26). In the Epistles, beginning with Romans 1:7 and ending with Jude 21, it is used frequently, as are variations of it. Interestingly, in the Book of Revelation neither it nor any variation of it is recorded until the closing verses (22:20–21).

Lord

The Greek word translated "Lord" is *kyrios*. "Lord" also translates the Hebrew word *ʾAdōnāy*. Both the Greek and Hebrew words include the idea of power or authority and signify mastery or ownership (Matt. 20:8; Mark 13:35). As a result they were used as a title of respect in addressing masters (e.g., Matt. 13:27), public officials (27:63), and teachers (John 4:11), and are sometimes translated "Sir." When the disciples addressed Jesus as "Lord," they were recognizing His deity (e.g., Matt. 8:25; 14:30), but it was also a title of respect (e.g., 18:21). In the Old Testament the word *Lord* also translates the Hebrew word *Yahweh*, the personal name of God. In many English versions it is printed in capital letters, LORD (e.g., Gen. 2:4). In the Acts of the Apostles and the rest of the New Testament, when Jesus is spoken of or addressed as Lord, His deity clearly is in mind (e.g., Acts 9:5–6; Rom. 10:9; 1 Cor. 4:4–5; Heb. 1:10). Variations such as "the Lord" (Mark 11:3; John 21:7, 12), "my Lord" (John 20:13), and "Lord Jesus" (e.g., Acts 4:33; Rom. 14:14) also refer to His deity. In the Old Testament, Jeremiah referred to Christ as "the LORD [Yahweh] Our Righteousness" (Jer. 23:6; 33:16); that is, He is the Source of righteousness available to believers.

Jesus

For Christians the chorus correctly states that "Jesus is the sweetest name I know." It is the Lord's given name and is the English transliteration of the Greek *Iēsous*. This in turn transliterates the Hebrew *Yᵉhôšūaʿ* (shortened form *Yᵉšūaʿ*), translated "Joshua." It means "He whose salvation is Yahweh" or "Yahweh's salvation." It was the name of Moses' lieutenant (Num. 11:28) and successor (Deut. 31:14, 23; 34:9), who led the Israelites into Canaan and conquered it (Josh. 1:1–6). The name "Jesus" was assigned to Him by God in the angel's appearance to Joseph in a dream (Matt. 1:20) "because he will save his people from their sins" (1:21). Because it was a popular name as a result of Joshua's significance in Israel's history, our Lord was frequently called "Jesus of Nazareth" (26:71; Mark 1:24; Luke 18:37; John 1:45; Acts 2:22) to distinguish Him from others named Jesus (e.g., Col. 4:11).

Christ

This title for Jesus is a transliteration of the Greek word *Christos,* which translates the Hebrew word *mᵉšîah,* Messiah, the "Anointed One." In Judaism "the tabernacle and everything in it" (Lev. 8:10) were anointed, as were Aaron as high priest and his sons as priests (Lev. 8:12, 30). Later, when God provided kings for Israel in response to their desires, the kings were anointed (1 Sam. 10:1; 16:12–13). The word was used prophetically in the Old Testament to speak of a promised Deliverer, who was to fulfill God's plans for Israel and all mankind (Ps. 2:2–9; Isa. 61:1–3; Dan. 9:25–26). When Jesus was on earth people anticipated the coming of the Messiah, that is, the Anointed One (John 4:25; 7:27b), and Jesus claimed to be that Christ (John 4:26; Luke 4:17–21). Andrew referred to Jesus as the Messiah (John 1:41), who is variously called "Christ" (Matt. 1:16), "the Christ" (Matt. 16:16, 20), and "Jesus Christ" (Mark 1:1; Acts 3:6).

VARIATIONS OF THE TITLE "SON"

Numerous names and titles involving variations of the word "Son" are given to Jesus, almost exclusively in the New Testament. Many of them point to His relationship to humanity. For example, in tracing Jesus' genealogy as far as His legal father, Joseph, is concerned, Matthew called him "the son of David" and "the son of Abraham" (Matt. 1:1). As the ultimate Descendant of David, Jesus is called "a shoot . . . from the stump of Jesse" (Isa. 11:1), "the Root of Jesse" (11:10), "a Righteous Branch" (Jer. 23:5; 33:15), "the Root of David" (Rev. 5:5), and "the Root and the Offspring of David" (22:16).

Because of this legal family relationship Jesus was called "Joseph's son" (Luke 4:22) and "the carpenter's son" (Matt. 13:55). Luke began his genealogy by writing that Jesus "was the son, so it was thought, of Joseph" (Luke 3:23), and Matthew closed his genealogy by identifying Joseph as "the husband of Mary, of whom was born Jesus" (Matt. 1:16). So because of Jesus' virgin birth, Joseph was Jesus' legal father but not His physical father.

In His hometown of Nazareth people spoke of Him as "the carpenter" and "Mary's son" (Mark 6:3). This mother-son relationship is referred to several other times in the New Testament. The angel told Joseph to "take

Mary home as your wife, because what is conceived in her is from the Holy Spirit. She will give birth to a son" (Matt. 1:20–21). Joseph did, and he "had no union with her until she gave birth to a son" (1:25). Likewise the angel Gabriel told Mary, "you will be with child and give birth to a son" (Luke 1:31). In Bethlehem Mary "gave birth to her firstborn, a son" (2:7). Elizabeth told Mary, "Blessed is the child you will bear" (1:42), and called her "the mother of my Lord" (1:43). Mary is called "the mother of Jesus" (Acts 1:14), "Jesus' mother" (Luke 8:19; John 2:3), "your mother" (Luke 8:20), and frequently "his mother" (Matt. 2:11, 13–14, 20–21; 12:46–47; see Mark 3:31–35; Luke 2:48, 51).

Son of God

The title "Son of God" was first applied to Jesus by the angel Gabriel in his announcement to the Virgin Mary. Explaining that her conception would be by the Holy Spirit, he said that "the holy one to be born will be called the Son of God" (Luke 1:35; see v. 32). John the Baptist, after witnessing the descent of the Holy Spirit on Jesus at His baptism by John, said, "I testify that this is the Son of God" (John 1:34). This was also the confession of Nathanael (1:49); of Martha, the sister of Lazarus and Mary (11:27); and of Peter, spokesman for the disciples (Matt. 16:15–16; see 14:33). When the earthquake occurred at Jesus' crucifixion, the centurion and soldiers who carried out the execution "were terrified, and exclaimed, 'Surely he was the Son of God'" (27:54; see Mark 15:39; Luke 23:47).

Significantly the demons, minions of Satan, whom Jesus exorcised in numerous healing miracles, recognized and addressed Jesus as the "Son of God" (Matt. 8:29; Mark 3:11; Luke 4:41; see 8:28, "Jesus, Son of the Most High God"). Even Satan himself acknowledged Jesus as the Son of God when he said, "If you are the Son of God" (Matt. 4:3, 6). In Greek this word "if" introduces a condition that assumes the statement to be true, and therefore can be translated "Since [or, assuming] you are the Son of God." Only the Son of God could turn stones into bread or cast Himself down from the highest point of the temple and have God protect Him from injury.

The closest Jesus came to directly calling Himself the Son of God occurred when the Jewish Sanhedrin asked Him, "'Are you then the Son of God?'" and Jesus replied, "'You are right in saying I am'" (Luke 22:70; see Matt. 26:63–64; Mark 14:61–62). Jesus did claim a close, unique relationship with God as His Father that amounted to His saying, "'I am God's Son'" (John 10:36; see vv. 29–30, 37–38). The first declaration of this relationship came when Jesus as a lad of twelve told Joseph and Mary when they found Him in the temple, "Didn't you know I had to be in my Father's house?" (Luke 2:49).

In claiming identity as God's Son on earth, Jesus emphasized His submission to God the Father's will and work. He told the Jews who persecuted Him for healing on the Sabbath, "I tell you the truth, the Son can do nothing by himself; he can do only what he sees the Father doing, because whatever the Father does the Son also does" (John 5:19). At the same time, however, Jesus' relationship with God the Father involved their equality in nature (10:30). After Jesus healed a man on the Sabbath, He said to the Jews, "My Father is always at his work to this very day, and I, too, am working" (5:17). Then they "tried all the harder to kill him," because "he was even calling God his own Father, making himself equal with God" (5:18). Nothing could be a clearer statement of His affirmation of deity. True, Jesus and God the Father are one in purpose, but John 5:17–18 and 10:30 affirm more than that: Christ is also equal to the Father in that Jesus possesses deity, the very essence of the Godhead.

Jesus' unique relationship to God the Father is underscored by His speaking repeatedly of God as "my Father" (e.g., Matt. 7:21; 18:10, 19, 35; Luke 10:22; 22:29; 24:49; John 5:43; 12:26–28; 14:2, 20–21, 23, 31; 15:1, 10, 15, 23–24; 16:25, 32). By contrast Jesus told His disciples to address God as "Our Father" (Matt. 6:9; see Luke 11:2), and in speaking to them He called God "your Father" (Matt. 10:20; 18:14; Mark 11:25; Luke 12:30–32; John 20:17).

Peter affirmed that Jesus is "the Christ, the Son of the living God" (Matt. 16:16). Interestingly the high priest asked Jesus, "Are you the Christ, the Son of the Blessed One?" (Mark 14:61). This is especially noteworthy since "Blessed One" is a Jewish substitute term for "God" (see Mishnah Berak'ot 7.3).

My Son, Whom I Love

Jesus' claim to be the Son of God was confirmed in a unique way by God the Father Himself. At Jesus' baptism by John the Baptist, which marked the beginning of Jesus' messianic ministry, God spoke from heaven, saying, "You are my Son, whom I love; with you I am well pleased" (Mark 1:11; see Matt. 3:17; Luke 3:22). Similarly, at Jesus' transfiguration on the mountain, God spoke to Peter, James, and John, saying, "This is my Son, whom I love; with him I am well pleased." Then God added, for the three disciples and for us as well, "Listen to him!" (Matt. 17:5; see Luke 9:35). Because of this unique relationship confirmed by God from heaven, John called Jesus "the one and only Son" (John 1:14; 3:16, 18; see 1:18, "the only Son"). In Psalm 2:7, quoted in Hebrews 1:5, God the Father called Jesus "my Son," and the words "in whom I delight" are from Isaiah 42:1.

Some Bible teachers have suggested that Jesus *became* the Son of God in His incarnation. In other words, He was not God's Son in eternity past before He became incarnate. This view has several weaknesses. First, it ignores clear statements in the Scriptures about Jesus' existence as the Son of God before the Incarnation. Galatians 4:4, for example, states that the Incarnation occurred "when the time had fully come," implying that the "Actor" was waiting in the wings for the appropriate moment of His appearance. The verse continues, "God sent his Son." The verb translated "sent" is coupled with a preposition that more literally could be translated "sent out from," again implying that He was the Son of God before He was incarnated. The same exact form of that verb is used in verse 6, which says, "God sent the Spirit of his Son"; the Spirit obviously came from heaven. Other Scriptures also speak of God sending His Son (1 John 4:9–10, 14), using a compound verb that literally could be translated "sent away from," implying preexistence with God the Father. And dozens of times the Gospel of John records that God "sent" His Son from heaven. Not one verse in the Bible states that Jesus ever *became* God's Son. He always was His Son, from all eternity.

Jesus' own references to His relationship with God the Father prior to the Incarnation are also significant. In His high priestly prayer Jesus requested, "And now, Father, glorify me in your presence with the glory I had with you before the world began" (John 17:5). Later He prayed concerning the disciples, "They knew with certainty that I came from you, and they believed that you sent me" (17:8b). Still later He stated that God the Father had "loved me before the creation of the world" (17:24b).

Another affirmation of Jesus' eternal Sonship is His participation in creation. The writer to the Hebrews stated that through His Son, God "made the universe" (Heb. 1:2). The Son, whom the Father "loves" (Col. 1:13), "is the image of the invisible God, the firstborn over all creation. For by him all things were created . . . all things were created by him and for him" (1:15–16).

The teaching that Jesus' Sonship began at the Incarnation ignores and destroys the eternal relationship among the three Persons of the Trinity, whereas the Bible clearly teaches the eternal distinctions in the Trinity as Father, Son, and Holy Spirit.

Son of Man

The title "Son of Man" occurs ninety-four times in the New Testament, eighty-nine of them by Jesus with reference to Himself in the four Gospels. In the Gospels others used this title of Him only when they referred to His own use of it. For example, they asked, "Who is this 'Son of Man'?" (John 12:34). Outside of the Gospels Stephen used the term "the Son of Man" in referring to the ascended glorified Jesus whom he saw in his vision just before he was martyred (Acts 7:55–56). Also the title was used by the author of Hebrews in quoting Psalm 8:5 (Heb. 2:7), and by the apostle John in his vision of the glorified Jesus standing among the seven lampstands representing the seven churches ("among the lampstands was someone 'like a son of man,'" Rev. 1:13) and in his vision of the Crowned One seated on a cloud with "a sharp sickle in his hand" (14:14).

Jesus' self-designation as "the Son of Man" (the first occurrence is in Matt. 8:20) may reflect the Aramaic use of the phrase as a substitute for "I," but it also obviously speaks of His humanity and His identity with humankind. Since the title was used repeatedly by God in addressing the prophet Ezekiel (e.g., Ezek. 2:1, 3, 6, 8), Jesus' use of it may serve to identify Him as a prophet, a fact recognized by the people (Matt. 21:11, 46;

Mark 6:15; Luke 7:16; 24:19b; John 4:19; 9:17) and claimed by Jesus (Matt. 13:57; Mark 6:4; Luke 4:24).

Since the title had messianic significance as a result of its occurrence in Daniel 7:13 as interpreted by subsequent Jewish scholars, Jesus' use of it was a claim to His identity as Israel's promised Messiah. This involved His ministry as the Suffering Servant and redemptive sacrifice (Matt. 20:28) who provides eternal life (John 6:53–58), accomplished by His death and resurrection at the end of His first coming. Jesus' exercise of "authority, glory, and sovereign power," His being worshiped by "all peoples, nations and men of every language," and His eternal kingdom and "everlasting dominion" (Dan. 7:14) will not be realized until His return to earth to establish His messianic kingdom, but Jesus was conscious of and spoke of His possession of those future messianic prerogatives (Matt. 16:27–28; 24:30; 26:64). At least some of those messianic rights were exercised by Jesus in His first coming, including the authority to forgive sins (9:6) and His authority over the Sabbath (12:8).

NAMES AND TITLES USED BY JESUS OF HIMSELF

In addition to calling Himself "the Son of Man," Jesus applied a number of descriptive titles to Himself, most of which are found in the Gospel of John and begin with "I am." This is significant in view of His words "I am" in John 8:58, an assertion of eternality and deity. The day after He miraculously fed the five thousand, Jesus challenged the people to work "for food that endures to eternal life, which the Son of Man will give you" (6:27), declaring, "I am the bread of life" (6:35, 48) and "I am the living bread that came down from heaven" (6:51).

At the Feast of Tabernacles Jesus attended in Jerusalem (John 7:14), He said to the people, "I am the light of the world" (8:12). This related to the practice of "lighting giant lamps in the women's court in the temple... . The wicks were made from the priest's worn-out garments."[1] Later Jesus repeated that declaration in His response to His disciples' question about the man born blind (9:1–4). Still later Jesus said, "I have come into the world as a light" (12:46). The apostle John called Jesus "the true light" (1:9; see 1:4–8).

Another custom the Jews observed at the Feast of Tabernacles was to make "a solemn procession each day from the temple to the Gihon Spring. A priest filled a gold pitcher with water while the choir sang Isaiah 12:3. Then they returned to the altar and poured out the water."[2] Although Jesus never stated, "I am the living water," He did stand on the last day of the feast and proclaim loudly, "If any man is thirsty, let him come to me and drink" (John 7:37). Similarly at Jacob's well in Sychar Jesus told the Samaritan woman, "If you knew the gift of God and who it is that asks you for a drink, you would have asked him and he would have given you living water" (4:10).

In discussing with the Jews His care for them as sheep, Jesus declared, "I am the gate for the sheep" (John 10:7) and "I am the gate; whoever enters through me will be saved" (10:9). To carry the analogy forward, Jesus identified Himself not only as the gate into the sheepfold but also as "the good shepherd" (10:11, 14). Jesus said that as the Good Shepherd He would lay down his life for the sheep (10:11, 15, 17–18). He also knows and cares for His sheep, keeping them from harm and providing for their needs. The New Testament writers built on this claim, calling Him "that great Shepherd of the sheep" (Heb. 13:20) and "the Chief Shepherd" (1 Pet. 5:4; see 2:25).

When Jesus went to Bethany, a village adjoining Jerusalem, to restore Lazarus to life, He comforted Martha, one of Lazarus' sisters, by saying, "Your brother will rise again" (John 11:23). When she responded that she knew Lazarus would "rise again in the resurrection at the last day" (11:24), Jesus declared, "I am the resurrection and the life" (11:25). As Jesus went on to explain, He is the Source of eternal life, and as a result, the Source of resurrection for all who believe in Him (11:25–26; see 5:21, 24–26, 28).

Jesus' announcement to His disciples that He would be leaving them and returning to His "Father's house . . . to prepare a place" (14:2) for them disturbed the disciples. His statement that they knew "the way to the place" where He was going (14:4) brought Thomas's response, "Lord, we don't know where you are going, so how can we know the way?" (14:5). To this, Jesus replied, "I am the way and the truth and the life" (14:6). To emphasize His exclusiveness as the only way to God, Jesus continued, "No one comes to the Father except through me." Building on this declaration the author of Hebrews wrote, "We have confidence to enter the Most Holy Place by the blood of Jesus, by a new and living way opened for us through the curtain, that is, his body" (Heb. 10:19–20).

As Jesus continued His instructions to the disciples, He spoke of the coming ministry of the "the Spirit of truth" (14:17), whom He called "another Counselor" (14:16; see 14:26; 15:26; 16:7). The Greek word rendered "Counselor" means a person "called to one's aid" (in a judicial sense), and thus may be translated "an advocate, pleader, intercessor."[3] Jesus did not directly declare, "I am a Counselor." But when He called the Holy Spirit "another Counselor," He meant "another of the same kind." In effect, therefore, He was identifying Himself as the Counselor who would soon be replaced by the Holy Spirit. As a result the apostle John identified Jesus as the "one who speaks to the Father in our defense" (1 John 2:1) when a Christian sins. "Wonderful Counselor" is one of the titles Isaiah assigned to Jesus (Isa. 9:6).

To emphasize the spiritual intimacy that needed to exist between Himself and His disciples to ensure their effective ministry, Jesus declared, "I am the true vine" (John 15:1) and "I am the vine; you are the branches" (15:5). With this claim Jesus was contrasting Himself with Israel, which "yielded only bad fruit" (Isa. 5:2). In addition to these seven "I am" titles, Jesus also called Himself "the Lord of the Sabbath" (Matt. 12:8; Luke 6:5), "Master" (Matt. 23:8), and "Teacher" (23:10; Mark 14:14).

NAMES AND TITLES GIVEN TO JESUS BY OTHERS

Of all the names and titles given to Jesus by other persons perhaps one of the more significant is "Immanuel—which means, 'God with us'" (Matt. 1:23; see Isa. 7:14). This was mentioned by the angel in his announcement to Joseph of the son to be born to Mary. It identifies Him as the Promised One (Isa. 7:14; 8:8) and affirms His deity as well as His humanity and earthly ministry. In the angel Gabriel's announcement to Mary, he said her son would be called "the Son of the Most High" (Luke 1:32) and "the holy one" (1:35). In addressing the women at the tomb after the resurrection the angel called Him "Jesus the Nazarene" (Mark 16:6; see Matt. 2:23).

During His earthly ministry Jesus was addressed as "Rabbi" by His disciples as well as by some who sought His help. The first use of this title was by two disciples of John the Baptist—one of whom was Andrew (John 1:40). Leaving John to follow Jesus, they said, "Rabbi, where are you staying?" (John 1:38).

Later Nathanael also addressed Jesus as "Rabbi" as well as "the King of Israel" (John 1:49) in response to Jesus' demonstration of His divine omnipresence and omniscience (1:47–48). On several occasions the disciples as a group addressed Jesus as "Rabbi" (John 4:31; 9:2; 11:8). Others who also addressed Him this way include Peter (Mark 9:5; 11:21), Judas Iscariot (Matt. 26:25, 49: Mark 14:45), Nicodemus (John 3:2), and the crowd of people whom Jesus had fed (6:25). In addition Mary Magdalene called Jesus "Rabboni" ("my Rabbi") after His resurrection (20:16). Bartimaeus too addressed Him as "Rabboni" (Mark 10:51, NKJV), though some manuscripts read "Rabbi."

Titles similar to "Rabbi" applied to Jesus are "Teacher" ("Rabbi" is sometimes translated "Teacher") and "Master." The title "Teacher" is used by Jesus' disciples (Mark 4:38; 9:38; 10:35; 13:1; Luke 21:7); individuals seeking His help (Mark 5:35; 9:17) or advice (Mark 10:17, 20); individuals commending Him (Matt. 8:19; Mark 12:32); and Pharisees, Sadducees, and other Jewish leaders who opposed Him (Matt. 12:38; 22:36; Mark 12:14, 19; Luke 7:40; 10:25; 12:14; 19:39). The word "Master" is found exclusively in Luke and is used only by Jesus' disciples (5:5; 8:24, 45; 9:33, 49) except on one occasion (17:13) when ten lepers sought His healing. *Epistata,* the Greek word rendered "Master," means "a leader" and thus suggests Jesus' authority.[4]

A significant title applied to Jesus in the New Testament is that of "Servant," used by Peter in his message to the crowd after he healed the crippled man (Acts 3:13, 26), and in the prayer of the disciples after Peter and John's release by the Sanhedrin (4:27, 30). It was picked up by the apostle Paul in his description of the "emptying" of Christ Jesus (Phil. 2:7–8). The Servant concept lies behind John the Baptist's identification of Jesus as "the Lamb of God, who takes away the sin of the world!" (John 1:29, 36; see Isa. 52:13–53:12). Although the Lord Jesus never referred to Himself as God's Servant, that concept lay behind His several dozen references to His being sent by the Father to do the Father's will and the work the Father gave Him to do (e.g., John 4:34; 5:30, 36; 6:38; 8:28–29; 12:49–50; 17:4).

Although He never directly called Himself a prophet, Jesus implied that He was one when He spoke of His being rejected in Nazareth, His hometown: "only in his home town and in his own house is a prophet without honor" (Matt. 13:57; see Mark 6:4; Luke 4:24; John 4:44). And the common people clearly considered Him a prophet (Matt. 21:11, 46; see Mark 6:15; Luke 7:16; 24:19; John 4:19; 7:40; 9:17). When Jesus asked His disciples who the people said He was, one of their replies was "one of the prophets" (Matt. 16:14; Mark 8:28).

When people on two occasions called Him "the Prophet" (John 6:14; 7:40), they had in mind Moses' statement, "The LORD your God will raise up for you a prophet like me from among your own brothers. You must listen to him" (Deut. 18:15; see Acts 3:22; 7:37). When asked by the Jews from Jerusalem, "Are you the Prophet?" John the Baptist emphatically answered "No" (John 1:21), but he implied that the person coming after him whom he would announce—that is, Jesus—would be the Prophet.

Besides being called a prophet, Jesus also has several regal titles: "Prince of Peace" (Isa. 9:6), "King" (Jer. 23:5; Zech. 14:9), "Ruler over Israel" (Mic. 5:2), "the king of the Jews" (Matt. 27:37; Mark 15:26; Luke 23:3, 38; John 19:19), "the Deliverer" (Rom. 11:26; see Isa. 59:20), "the ruler of the kings of the earth" (Rev. 1:5), "the ruler of God's creation" (3:14); "King of the ages" (15:3), and "King of kings and Lord of lords" (17:14; 19:16).

In addition, Jesus is the believers' "high priest" (Heb. 2:17; 3:1; 4:15; 5:10; 6:20; 9:11), "great high priest" (4:14), "great priest" (10:21), and "priest" (5:6; 7:3, 17, 21; 10:12). In this priestly capacity, He is the "Mediator" between God and humanity (1 Tim. 2:5).

The title "Savior," often used of Christ, points to the purpose of His incarnation—to bring salvation to mankind. Hearing the Samaritan women's words about Jesus, the people of the town of Samaria said, "We know that this man really is the Savior of the world" (John 4:42). Later John wrote that Jesus is "the Savior of the world" (1 John 4:14). The title "Savior" is often combined with other titles: "the Savior Jesus" (Acts 13:23); "our Savior, Jesus Christ" (2 Tim. 1:10); "Christ Jesus our Savior" (Titus 1:4); "God and Savior Jesus Christ" (Titus 2:13; 2 Pet. 1:1); "Jesus Christ our Savior" (Titus 3:6); "our Lord and Savior Jesus Christ" (2 Pet. 2:20; 3:18); and "our Lord and Savior" (2 Pet. 3:2).

Just as lambs on the Jewish Passover were sacrificed to deal with the people's sins, so Jesus was sacrificed on the cross to atone for sin. As such He was called "the Lamb of God" (John 1:29, 36) and "our Passover Lamb" (1 Cor. 5:7).

As the Savior sent from God as the Father's representative, Jesus is called "the apostle," that is, the One sent from God the Father with delegated authority (Heb. 3:1).

Paul called Jesus Christ "the image of God" (2 Cor. 4:4) and "the image of the invisible God" (Col. 1:15), that is, the exact reflection and representation of God the Father (Heb. 1:3). Since the Father is invisible (John 1:18; 5:37; 6:46; 1 Tim. 1:17; 1 John 4:12), Jesus has revealed Him to humanity (John 1:18). He is God's "firstborn" (Rom. 8:29; Heb. 1:6; 12:23), and Paul said Jesus is "the firstborn over all creation" (Col. 1:15). This does not mean, as some cultists suggest, that He was created by God the Father, but that He, like the firstborn son in a family, holds the place of prominence as the "heir of all things" (Heb. 1:2).

As "the beginning" (Col. 1:18), He is the creative Origin of all things. And as "the Beginning and the End" (Rev. 21:6; 22:13), He is the Source and the culmination of all creation.

Because Christ is the first one ever to receive a resurrected body, Paul called Him "the firstborn from the dead" (Col. 1:18). The apostle John also spoke of Jesus as "the firstborn from the dead" (Rev. 1:5). In farming, the first crops to be harvested were called "firstfruits" (Lev. 23:10–11), an indication that more crops were to follow. Similarly in Jesus' resurrection He is "the firstfruits" of the dead (1 Cor. 15:20), which means His followers will also be resurrected. As "the firstborn from among the dead" (Col. 1:18), He is the Heir of all who will be resurrected to eternal life.

A clear, forthright affirmation of Jesus' deity is given in Hebrews 1:8. Speaking of Jesus, the writer quoted Psalm 45:6, "Your throne, O God, will last forever and ever." Another direct claim of His deity, in which Jesus is called God, is in Romans 9:5: "Christ, who is God over all." Another is in Titus 2:13, in which Jesus is called "our great God." And Isaiah titled Him "Mighty God" and "Everlasting Father" (Isa. 9:6). The title

"Everlasting Father" does not mean Jesus the Son is to be confused with God the Father. Instead the term refers to Jesus' fatherly compassion, protection, and provisions, similar to that of a caring earthly father.

Acknowledging His deity, Peter called Jesus "the Holy and Righteous One" (Acts 3:14), and Stephen, Ananias, and John spoke of Him as "the Righteous One" (7:52; 22:14; 1 John 2:1).

The apostle John used numerous titles of Jesus, including "the Word" (John 1:1, 14); "the Word of life" (1 John 1:1); "Advocate" (2:1, NKJV); "the Word of God" (Rev. 19:13); "the faithful witness" (1:5); "the Alpha and the Omega" (1:8; 21:6; 22:13, the first and last letters of the Greek alphabet, which express His fullness); "the First and the Last" (1:17; 2:8; 22:13); "the Beginning and the End" (21:6; 22:13); "the Faithful and True" (19:11); "the Lion of the tribe of Judah"(5:5); and "the Lamb"(5:8, 12–13; 6:1, 3, 5, 7, 16; 7:9–10, 14, 17; 12:11; 13:8; 14:1, 4 [twice], 10; 15:3; 17:14 [twice]; 19:7, 9; 21:9, 14, 22–23, 27; 22:1, 3).

A number of titles applied to Jesus relate Him to those who believe on Him, more particularly to the church. The first of these is "Author," also translated "Prince" (Acts 5:31). The Greek word *archēgos* means "one who begins or originates," or, with reference to a person, a "founder, author, prince, leader."[5] Peter told the Jews in the temple area that they "killed the author of life" (3:15), speaking of Jesus. The writer of Hebrews called Jesus "the author of their salvation" (Heb. 2:10) and "the author and perfecter of our faith" (12:2).

Another title that relates the Lord Jesus to the church is Bridegroom. John the Baptist applied this title to Jesus when he explained to his disciples, "The bride belongs to the bridegroom. The friend who attends the bridegroom waits and listens for him, and is full of joy when he hears the bridegroom's voice. That joy is mine, and it is now complete" (John 3:29). Jesus in effect applied the title to Himself when He explained why His disciples were not fasting. "How can the guests of the bridegroom fast while he is with them? They cannot, so long as they have him with them. But the time will come when the bridegroom will be taken from them, and on that day they will fast" (Mark 2:19–20). Jesus' parables of the wedding banquet (Matt. 22:1–10) and of the ten virgins and the wedding feast (25:1–13) also allude to His identity as the Bridegroom. Related to this picture are the references to Christ and His church as husband and wife (2 Cor. 11:2; Eph. 5:22–33; Rev. 19:7–9; 21:9; 22:17).

A graphic title that relates Jesus Christ to His church is that of "the head of the body, the church" (Col. 1:18). Paul stated that "God . . . appointed him to be head over everything for the church, which is his body" (Eph. 1:22–23). Believers are encouraged to "grow up into him who is the Head, that is Christ" (4:15; see Col. 2:19), and Christ as "the head of the church, his body" is the example for husbands as "head of the wife" (Eph. 5:23). Several passages refer to the church as Christ's body and to believers as members of that body (Rom. 7:4; 12:4–5; 1 Cor. 12:12–14, 27; Eph. 2:15b–16; 4:4; Col. 1:24; 3:15). This analogy portrays the intimacy of relationship between the Lord Jesus and believers and the relationship among believers.

Jesus Christ is also identified as the Stone. In relation to Israel, Jesus is "a stone that causes men to stumble and a rock that makes them fall" (Isa. 8:14). In discussing the Jews' unbelief Paul wrote, "They stumbled over the stumbling stone," and then he quoted Isaiah 8:14 (Rom. 9:33–34; see 1 Pet. 2:8). Psalm 118:22 is related to Israel's unbelief and God's building on it: "The stone the builders rejected has become the capstone." Jesus quoted this passage and related it to Himself in His discussion with the Jewish leaders in the temple courts shortly before His crucifixion (Matt. 21:42; see Mark 12:10; Luke 20:17). Also Peter quoted it when he addressed the Sanhedrin (Acts 4:11), and in his first epistle (1 Pet. 2:7).

Peter developed the picture of the Lord Jesus as a stone more fully than anyone else. He described Jesus as "the living Stone—rejected by men but chosen by God and precious to him" (1 Pet. 2:4). He continued the picture by describing believers as "living stones . . . being built into a spiritual house" (2:5), and then quoted Isaiah 28:16 loosely: "See, I lay in Zion, a chosen and precious cornerstone, and the one who trusts in him will never be put to shame" (2:6). Paul also referred to Jesus Christ "as the chief cornerstone" in whom "the whole building" of believers "is joined together and rises to become a holy temple in the Lord" (Eph. 2:20–21).

Peter also called Jesus an "Overseer of your souls" (1 Pet. 2:25). In this role He lovingly watches over and directs the lives of His own.

The fact that so many names and titles exist to describe the Lord Jesus underscores both the fullness and the complexity of His person. (The following table lists 108 titles discussed in this chapter.) Just as the multitude of facets in a diamond increases its brilliance, so the many names and titles of Christ reveal Him as "the radiance of God's glory" (Heb. 1:3).

Titles and Names of Jesus Christ*

Lord Jesus Christ	Son of Man
Lord	Bread of Life
My Lord	Light of the World
Lord Jesus	True Light
The LORD Our Righteousness	Gate
Jesus	Good Shepherd
Jesus of Nazareth	Great Shepherd
Christ	Chief Shepherd
Messiah ("the Anointed One")	Resurrection
Jesus Christ	Way
Son of David	Truth
Son of Abraham	Life
A Shoot	Wonderful Counselor
Root of Jesse	Vine
Righteous Branch	True Vine
Root of David	Lord of the Sabbath
Root and Offspring of David	Master
Joseph's son	Teacher
The Carpenter's son	Immanuel
Carpenter	Son of the Most High
Mary's son	Holy One
Son of God	Jesus the Nazarene
Son of the Most High God	Rabbi
Son of the Living God	King of Israel
Son of the Blessed One	Rabboni
My Son	Servant
One and Only Son	Lamb of God
Only Son	Prophet

Prince of Peace	God
King	Everlasting Father
Ruler over Israel	Holy and Righteous One
King of the Jews	Righteous One
Deliverer	Word
Ruler of the kings of the earth	Word of life
Ruler of God's creation	Advocate
King of the ages	Word of God
King of kings and Lord of lords	Faithful Witness
High Priest	Alpha
Great High Priest	Omega
Great Priest	First
Priest	Last
Mediator	Faithful and True
Savior of the world	Lion of the tribe of Judah
Savior	Lord
Our Passover Lamb	Author
Apostle	Prince
Image of God	Author and Perfector of our
Image of the invisible God	faith
Firstborn	Bridegroom
Firstborn of all creation	Head of the church
Heir	Stone
Beginning	Cornerstone
End	Chief Cornerstone
Firstborn from the dead	Overseer
Firstfruits	

*These titles are listed in the order in which they were discussed in this chapter.

Five

THE INCARNATION OF THE SON
OF GOD ANNOUNCED

⟨divider⟩

People have always been intrigued, it seems, with the question of whether living beings inhabit other planets and have visited the earth. Half a century ago Orson Wells temporarily threw much of the United States into turmoil with his radio broadcast simulation of an invasion from Mars. As both the century and the millennium draw to a close, this fascination increases, and much of it is bizarre. The Bible makes it clear that God's hosts of angels inhabit the heavens (Mark 12:25; 13:32; Eph. 3:10) with access to the earth in ministry for God (Gen. 28:12–13; Luke 2:13–15; John 1:51). Angels, however, are spirit beings (Heb. 1:14) with powers to assume bodily form to appear and to minister to people (Gen. 18:1–19: 21; Matt. 28:2–7; Acts 1:10–11) but without an inherent bodily form. As a result, the incarnation of our Lord Jesus Christ is the first and only time someone has come from heaven and identified himself with humanity.

In *Mere Christianity* C. S. Lewis entitles his chapter on the Incarnation "The Invasion." Perhaps a more accurate description would be "the infiltration," because, as Lewis writes, "Enemy-occupied territory—that is what this world is. Christianity is the story of how the rightful king has landed, you might say landed in disguise, and is calling us to take part in a great campaign of sabotage."[1] God, nonetheless, has announced a number of times the incarnation of His Son and the birth of His Son's forerunner as well.

THE JESUS SEMINAR AND
THE SEARCH FOR THE HISTORICAL JESUS

Before discussing the biblical evidence concerning the incarnation of the eternal Son of God, His person as the God-Man, and His earthly life and ministry, it is important to discuss the search for the historical Jesus that has marked liberal biblical studies for the last couple of centuries. Of significance is the "Jesus Seminar," a continuing search since 1985 for what the historical Jesus said and did. This study is being carried on "under the auspices of the Westar Institute."[2] The primary leader of the Jesus Seminar is Robert W. Funk, assisted by cochairman John Dominic Crossan. The first meeting of thirty scholars was held March 21–24, 1985, at St. Meinrad School of Theology, a Roman Catholic seminary in southern Indiana. Since that time it has met semiannually at different locations with a total of two hundred individuals involved in one way or another. Its definitive production, *The Five Gospels: In Search of the Authentic Words of Jesus*, edited by Robert W. Funk, Roy W. Hoover, and the Jesus Seminar (New York: Macmillan, 1993) lists seventy Fellows.

In some respects the search for the historical Jesus is the product of the Reformation, which is in part the product of the Renaissance. More specifically the search for the historical Jesus is the product of the Enlightenment with its emphasis on rationalism and the scientific method. This involved the rejection of God's intervention in this world and human affairs—the denial of the miraculous—as represented by Deism. "In other words," as Robert Strimple points out, "the starting point of the modern quest of the historical Jesus is the assumption that the Jesus presented in our biblical gospels is not the Jesus of history."[3]

Hermann Samuel Reimarus (1694–1768) is generally acknowledged as the father of the "search" for the historical Jesus. Its beginning is pinpointed to 1778 with the posthumous publication of his Wolfbüttel Fragment entitled "Concerning the Aims of Jesus and His Disciples." Other leaders include David Friedrich Strauss, with the publication of his *Life of*

Jesus Critically Examined (1835), Johannes Weiss with his *Jesus' Procla-mation of the Kingdom of God* (1892), and Albert Schweitzer with *The Quest for the Historical Jesus* (1906).

The major difference between the older quest for the historical Jesus and the quest identified with the Jesus Seminar lies in their basic attitudes toward the study of the Gospels. The older critics were seeking to identify and eliminate what was not historical (i.e., the supernatural and miracu-lous) from what was basically considered a historical record of Jesus' ministry. The Jesus Seminar, on the contrary, is seeking to discover what is historical in what is assumed to be essentially unhistorical. It is not surprising, as a result, that "eighty-two percent of the words ascribed to Jesus in the gospels were not actually spoken by him, according to the Jesus Seminar."[4]

The rules of evidence formulated and adopted by the Jesus Seminar "to guide its assessment of gospel tradition"[5] lack substantiation from other sources and are therefore highly suspect. The first, for example, is that "the evidence provided by the written gospels is hearsay evidence . . . secondhand evidence," because none of the authors of the Gospels "was an ear or eyewitness of the words and events he records."[6] This assumes that Matthew and John did not write the Gospels attributed to them—a highly questionable conclusion. It also rejects the promise of Jesus to the Eleven that the Holy Spirit would "bring to your remembrance all things that I said to you" (John 14:26, NKJV). It also rejects as invalid Luke's as-sertion that he wrote his Gospel only after "having investigated everything carefully from the beginning" so that Theophilus "might know the exact truth about the things you have been taught" (Luke 1:3–4, NASB).

The other rules of written evidence adopted by the Jesus Seminar simi-larly are assumed without substantiation. These include the idea that sayings of Jesus were brought together in clusters or were provided with a narrative context by the Gospel writers. Furthermore, according to the Jesus Seminar, the Gospel writers expanded the sayings or parables, added interpretive ma-terial, or revised them to conform to their own viewpoints. These authors also allegedly attributed to Jesus statements from common wisdom or their own statements. Jesus is identified as the Galilean "Sage" who "is self-effacing, modest, unostentatious,"[7] and anything in the Gospels that contradicts that picture is simply eliminated as not part of the historical Jesus.

Criticism of the Jesus Seminar and its methodology has come not just from theologically conservative evangelicals but also from Roman Catholics and theologically liberal Protestants. In the preface to his book *The Real Jesus* Luke Timothy Johnson characterizes the work of the Jesus Seminar as "a kind of second-rate scholarship" and "ersatz scholarship."[8] Later he quotes a number of leading New Testament scholars with critical evaluations of the Seminar and its findings, including Howard Clark Kee, who "declared the Seminar 'an academic disgrace.'"[9]

Johnson explains why he draws this conclusion about the Seminar and its pronouncements. "Like a great deal of Gospel criticism," he wrote, "it began with the assumption that the Gospels are not accurate histories but are narratives constructed out of traditional materials with literary art and theological motives."[10] He continued, "From the start, then, we see that the agenda of the Seminar is not disinterested scholarship, but a social mission against the way in which the church controls the Bible, and the way in which the church is dominated by a form of evangelical and eschatological theology—that is, a theology focused both on the literal truth of the Gospels and the literal return of Jesus."[11] With justification Johnson concluded that "any pretense the Seminar has maintained with regard to scientific discovery was . . . merely pretense: the results were already determined ahead of time. The goal was the construction of a new Gospel that portrayed a noneschatological and 'nonmythical' Jesus."[12]

Johnson also criticizes the Jesus Seminar for its methodology. "The Jesus Seminar's promise to deliver, by means of historical methods, 'the real Jesus' is, we have seen, fraudulent on two counts. The first is that its historical methodology is flawed. The second is that even the best historical reconstruction cannot supply 'the real Jesus,' any more than it can supply "the real Socrates." Historians can make a number of important, indeed critical assertions about Jesus' ministry, but the evidence provided by the ancient sources does not enable a satisfying reconstruction of it."[13]

Careful analysis and study of the Gospel records of the life and ministry of Jesus Christ is always appropriate, but to reject their accuracy and authenticity, which is supported by strong external evidence, in an effort to reconstruct His person, life, and ministry, as the Jesus Seminar does, is wrongheaded.

THE BIRTH OF THE FORERUNNER ANNOUNCED

John the Baptist is identified in the Gospel of Mark as the forerunner of Jesus Christ. To confirm John's ministry Mark quoted from Malachi 3:1 and Isaiah 40:3—the latter verse also being quoted by Matthew (3:3) and Luke (3:4) and by John himself (John 1:23). By revelation the apostle John described John the Baptist "as a witness to testify concerning that light, so that through him all men might believe. He himself was not the light; he came only as a witness to the light" (1:7–8). A forerunner was a precursor who announced coming royalty; this was John's ministry. When John's disciples complained to him about Jesus that "everyone is going to him," John reminded them, "You yourselves can testify that I said, 'I am not the Christ but am sent ahead of him'" (3:28).

The incarnation of Christ is unquestionably the supreme miracle—God joining Himself with humanity forever as the God-Man. It is fitting, therefore, from the human perspective that His human forerunner's conception also be a miracle and be announced by an angelic messenger. It is also fitting that Jesus' forerunner be a descendant of Aaron, brother of Moses and first high priest in Israel, through both his father Zechariah of "the priestly division of Abijah" (Luke 1:5) and his mother Elizabeth, since he would set Jesus apart to His public messianic ministry on earth (Matt. 3:13–17; John 1:29–34). The name of John's father, Zechariah, is also appropriate. It means "God remembers," something God was certainly doing in the birth of John and the incarnation of Jesus.

On one occasion when Zechariah's priestly "division was on duty and he was serving as priest before God," Luke related that "he was chosen by lot . . . to go into the temple of the Lord and burn incense" (Luke 1:8–9). The choice was by lot but it was not by chance; it is written of the lot that "its every decision is from the LORD" (Prov. 16:33). As Zechariah performed his duties, "an angel of the Lord appeared to him" (Luke 1:11), who later identified himself as Gabriel (1:19). The angel announced that, despite his wife Elizabeth's barrenness in her advanced age, his prayers for a son would be answered and she would conceive and bear a son, whose name was to be John (1:7, 13). This child was to be a Nazirite and would "be filled with the Holy Spirit even from birth" (1:15). In announcing John's birth, Gabriel in effect also announced the coming of God's Messiah, because he said that John "will go on before the Lord, in the spirit and power of Elijah [see Mal. 4:5; Matt. 11:14] . . . to make ready a people prepared for the Lord" (Luke 1:17).

Knowing of God's miraculous provision of Isaac to Abraham and Sarah when she was barren and beyond the age of conceiving and bearing a child (Gen. 18:9–15; 21:1–7), Zechariah should have trusted the angel's message; but, like many of us, he doubted God's revelation and asked, "How can I be sure of this? I am an old man and my wife is well along in years" (Luke 1:18). For his lack of faith Zechariah was struck dumb from that moment (1:20, 22, 62–65). In his song that followed his restored ability to speak, Zechariah understood and proclaimed the ministry of his son John as the forerunner of the Messiah (1:76).

THE VIRGIN CONCEPTION ANNOUNCED

Through the centuries Christians have spoken of the virgin birth of Jesus. This is part of the Roman Catholic Church's exaltation of Mary and its teaching that in Jesus' birth her virginity remained undisturbed and that she remained a virgin throughout her life even though she married Joseph. Actually the birth of Jesus was a completely normal human birth. It was His conception that was miraculous; He was conceived by God the Holy Spirit (Luke 1:35). It is because of this fact, not because Mary was "immaculate," that the angel Gabriel called Him "the holy one to be born" and "the Son of God" (1:35).

To Mary

The angel Gabriel, who told Zechariah of the birth of his son John, appeared next to a virgin named Mary who was "pledged to be married to a man named Joseph, a descendant of David" (Luke 1:27). This was in Nazareth, a town in Galilee, and occurred in the sixth month of the pregnancy of Zechariah's wife, Elizabeth. As with Zechariah, Gabriel told Mary, "Do not be afraid" (1:30; see v. 13), understandably a necessary statement when an angel appears! He also called Mary "highly favored" and told her, "The Lord is with you" (1:28) and "you have found favor with God" (1:30). Then he proceeded to tell her, "You will be with child and give birth to a son" to be named Jesus (1:31). This child would be called "the Son of the Most High" (1:32), the promised Messiah who would receive "the throne of his father David, and . . . reign over the house of Jacob forever" in an everlasting kingdom (1:32–33).

From Gabriel's opening statement it sounds as though Mary was being told what would happen without her having a choice to accept or reject the assignment. This is not true; human beings are not automatons, but God knew Mary's submissive spirit. Mary did ask, however, "How will this be . . . since I am a virgin?" (1:34). This question did not reflect lack of faith; it was simply a request for an explanation of the procedure. Gabriel explained that the child would be conceived by God the Holy Spirit and therefore He would be called "the Son of God" (1:35). To encourage Mary, Gabriel told her of her relative Elizabeth's divinely provided pregnancy. Mary undoubtedly was aware of the misunderstanding and accusation she would face, but her response to Gabriel and the Lord is a model for all believers—"I am the Lord's servant. . . . May it be to me as you have said" (1:38).

To Joseph

Although God loves and blesses godly single parents, He is the creator of marriage and the two-parent family (Gen. 1:27–28; 2:20–24). He needed, therefore, to inform Joseph, Mary's fiancé, of the nature of her situation. Joseph was also an integral part of the puzzle because he gave Jesus his legal right to the throne of David through Solomon (Matt. 1:6–16), while Mary, also a descendant of David through another son, Nathan, gave Jesus His physical right to the throne (Luke 3:23–31).

When Joseph first learned of Mary's pregnancy, he was not aware of its supernatural origin. As a result "he had a mind to divorce her quietly" because he "was a righteous man and did not want to expose her to public disgrace" (Matt. 1:19). This shows that Joseph genuinely loved Mary. At that point God sent an angel (whether Gabriel or not is not stated) to inform Joseph in a dream concerning Mary's part in the plan of God. He was instructed to "take Mary home as your wife" and to name her son

"Jesus, because he will save his people from their sins" (1:20–21). Like Mary, Joseph was obedient to the divine instructions and "took Mary home as his wife. But he had no union with her until she gave birth to a son" (1:24–25). This implies that Joseph and Mary enjoyed normal marital relations following the birth of Jesus, a fact supported by references to his brothers (Matt. 12:46–47; 13:55–56; John 2:12; 7:3; 5, 10; Acts 1:14). Thus the Bible does not support the Roman Catholic teaching of the perpetual virginity of Mary.

THE OCCURRENCE OF THE BIRTH OF JESUS

Joseph and Mary were living in Nazareth, a small town in Galilee, where Joseph worked as a carpenter (Luke 1:26–27). The Bible, however, had prophesied that Bethlehem, where David was born, would be the birthplace of "one who will be ruler over Israel" (Mic. 5:2), God's Messiah. God's control of the affairs of men and of nations to fulfill that prediction should encourage all believers to trust Him to carry out His program. Unaware of God's prompting, "Caesar Augustus issued a decree that a census should be taken of the entire Roman world. . . . And everyone went to his own town to register" (Luke 2:1, 3). As a result Joseph "went up from the town of Nazareth in Galilee to Judea, to Bethlehem the town of David, because he belonged to the house and line of David. He went there to register with Mary, who was pledged to be married to him and was expecting a child" (2:4–5). There in Bethlehem in exact fulfillment of God's prophecy "the time came for the baby to be born, and she gave birth to her firstborn, a son" (2:6–7).

Evidence that the incarnation of the Son of God was a quiet "infiltration," not an open "invasion," includes the fact that Mary placed the infant Jesus "in a manger, because there was no room for them in the inn" (2:7). The apostle John wrote, "He came to that which was his own, but his own did not receive him" (John 1:11). When Jesus first returned to His hometown of Nazareth, He ministered in the synagogue. Amazed by His teaching, the people asked, "Isn't this Joseph's son?" (Luke 4:22). When He rebuked them for their lack of faith, "all the people in the synagogue were furious" and "got up, drove him out of the town, and took him to the brow of the hill on which the town was built, in order to throw him down the cliff. But he walked right through the crowd and went on his way" (4:28–30). When He returned to Nazareth later, the people dismissed Him as "the carpenter's son" (Matt. 13:55), and "they took offense at him" (Mark 6:3).

THE ANNOUNCEMENT OF THE BIRTH OF JESUS

Proud parents send birth announcements of their children, their first-born in particular, to their extended family members and their friends. Proud fathers place in their front yard wooden storks festooned with balloons and a placard announcing the details. Some fathers try to find an unusual way to announce their child's birth. When my firstborn daughter arrived, I reproduced in miniature the birth certificate with her photograph and footprints on it, and sent it as the announcement. No one, however, ever has or ever will top the birth announcement of God the Father at the birth of His Son, our Lord Jesus Christ.

To the Shepherds

God announced the birth of Jesus to shepherds in the fields near Bethlehem, who were "keeping watch over their flocks at night" (Luke 2:8). This is appropriate because David had been a shepherd (1 Sam. 16:11–12; 17:14) and Jesus Christ called Himself "the good shepherd" who "lays down his life for the sheep" (John 10:11; see vv. 14–16). He was also called "that great Shepherd of the sheep" (Heb. 13:20), "the Shepherd and Overseer of your souls" (1 Pet. 2:25), and "the Chief Shepherd" (5:4). Numerous commentators suggest that these shepherds were caring for the sacrificial sheep for the temple sacrifices in Jerusalem. If that is true, it is appropriate that the birth announcement of "the Lamb of God, who takes away the sin of the world" (John 1:29; see v. 36)—and who thus ended the need for those sacrifices—was made to these shepherds. It also demonstrates God's interest in and concern for lowly people in this world (1 Cor. 1:27–29).

Luke reported that the announcement was made by "an angel of the Lord" (Luke 2:9). This angel, whose identity is not stated reported, "Today in the town of David a Savior has been born to you; he is Christ the Lord" (2:11). The identifying sign would be "a baby wrapped in cloth and lying in a manger" (2:12). As soon as the angel's announcement was given, "a great company of the heavenly host appeared with the angel, praising God and saying, 'Glory to God in the highest, and on earth peace to men on whom his favor rests'" (2:13–14). That was a birth announcement that will never be matched. It announced the birth of the eternal Son of God as a person joined forever with the human race as its Messiah, Savior, Ruler, and Judge. This announcement to the shepherds constituted, in effect, an announcement to the people of Israel.

To the Magi

God the Father also made an announcement of the birth of His Son to the Gentiles. Centuries earlier through Isaiah, God had said to His preincarnate Son, "It is too small a thing for you to be my servant to restore the tribes of Jacob and bring back those of Israel I have kept. I will also make you a light for the Gentiles, that you may bring my salvation to the ends of the earth" (Isa. 49:6; see 42:6; 51:4). No announcement is stated as such, but the Magi, when they came to Jerusalem and asked concerning "the one who has been born king of the Jews," said, "We saw his star in the east and have come to worship him" (Matt. 2:2). These men, astrologers and philosophers from Parthia, were part of a class of soothsayers that extended back at least to Daniel and his three friends (Dan. 1:3–6, 17–20). As a result the Magi evidently knew the Old Testament passages mentioning a star and the coming King of Israel (Num. 24:17; Isa. 60:1–3).

No one knows what this star was except that it announced the birth of God's Son. Efforts to identify it with an astronomical phenomenon focus on "an unidentified comet . . . a supernova [or] several planets [that] converged with a brilliant star,"[14] but a natural explanation is fruitless. W. White appropriately wrote, "A more acceptable alternative seems to be that God provided a source of light which cannot now be determined."[15] Apparently the star did not lead the Magi from their homes to Jerusalem; but when they left Jerusalem for Bethlehem (Matt. 2:4–8), "the star they had seen in the east went ahead of them until it stopped over the place where the child was. When they saw the star, they were overjoyed" (2:9–10). This shows that it was a supernatural provision from God.

The star apparently had first appeared and had been seen by the Magi in conjunction with the actual birth of Jesus in Bethlehem. The consultation of the Magi (traditionally thought to be three because three kinds of gifts were given to Jesus), their preparation of their caravan to make the journey through bandit-infested territory and the journey itself took time. As a result Jesus was no longer a newborn infant lying in a manger, as often depicted in Christmas pageants. The family of Joseph, Mary, and Jesus was living in a house (2:11), and Jesus is called "the child," the Greek word *paidion* signifying "a young child," not an infant *(brephos)*. When King Herod realized the Magi had returned to their homes without informing him of the child's location, "he gave orders to kill all the boys in Bethlehem and its vicinity who were two years old and under" (2:16). So Jesus then was obviously in this age range.

THE PROCLAMATION OF THE BIRTH OF JESUS

The announcements of the birth of Jesus were essentially private affairs. The Magi saw the star and interpreted it in conjunction with predictions in Jewish Scriptures. Although they reported the news to Herod and the Jewish leaders in Jerusalem, the news was still localized. The angelic announcement to the shepherds was at night so that, even though it was a brilliant display, it was witnessed only by them. After they confirmed the angel's message by finding Mary, Joseph, "and the baby . . . lying in the manger" (Luke 2:16), Luke wrote that "they spread the word concerning what had been told them about this child" (2:17); but this was a comparatively small number of people in the town of Bethlehem. A need existed for a public proclamation of the good news of the birth of Israel's Messiah.

By Simeon

As faithful Jews, Joseph and Mary had Jesus circumcised the eighth day (Lev. 12:3), and they named Him Jesus as Gabriel told Mary (Luke 1:31) and the angel told Joseph (Matt. 1:21). After waiting thirty-three additional days for Mary's purification according to the Law of Moses (Lev. 12:4), Joseph and Mary went to Jerusalem to the temple to present Jesus, their firstborn son, to the Lord (Exod. 13:2) and to offer the sacrifice of redemption for Him according to the Law of Moses (13:12–13). This sacrifice was to be a lamb, but those who could not afford a lamb could substitute "two doves or two young pigeons" (Lev. 12:8; see Luke 2:24). The fact that they brought the latter reveals Joseph and Mary's low economic level.

Simeon, a "righteous and devout person," was "waiting for the consolation of Israel, and the Holy Spirit was upon him" (Luke 2:25). He represented a godly remnant in that era of apostasy and formalism. God had revealed to him that "he would not die before he had seen the Lord's Christ" (2:26). When Joseph and Mary came into the temple with Jesus, Simeon, led by the Holy Spirit (2:27), took Jesus "into his arms, and praised God" (2:28). He declared his readiness now to depart in death, "for my eyes have seen your salvation, which you have prepared in the sight of all people, a light for revelation to the Gentiles and for glory to your people Israel" (2:30–32).

Simeon, who is never mentioned before or afterward in the Bible, then blessed Joseph and Mary and, as a prophet, spoke the following message concerning Jesus' incarnate life and ministry and Mary's future heartache: "This child is destined to cause the falling and rising of many in Israel, and to be a sign that will be spoken against, so that the thoughts of many hearts will be revealed. And a sword will pierce your own soul too" (2:34–35). Undoubtedly Simeon's actions and words were observed and heard by many in the crowded temple courts.

By Anna

Described as "a prophetess" (Luke 2:36), Anna is identified by her family and personal history. Widowed after seven years of marriage, she was then eighty-four years of age (2:36–37). Luke reported that "she never left the temple but worshiped night and day, fasting and praying" (2:37), evidence of her devotion to God. Approaching Joseph and Mary and Jesus as Simeon left, Anna "spoke about the child to all who were looking forward to the redemption of Jerusalem" (2:38). Through Simeon and Anna, public proclamation of the birth of God's Messiah was made to the people of Israel, and in particular to the devout and godly ones who were looking and praying for His promised coming.

Six

THE PERSON OF THE
INCARNATE SON OF GOD

═══◉═══

Our Lord Jesus Christ is a unique person, not in our contemporary watered-down sense of "unusual" but in the absolute meaning of "one of a kind." He is the theanthropic person, the God-Man. As such He is the permanent joining of the eternal Word, the second person of the triune Godhead, with humanity. As the revelatory person of the Godhead, the Word was eternally destined to become incarnate. The incarnation of the Word was not the result of the Trinity casting lots, with the Word happening to draw the short straw, nor was it a case of His being outvoted by God the Father and God the Holy Spirit; it was His mission as the Word, the expression of God, to manifest and display God in human form. The apostle John stated, "No one has ever seen God, but God the One and Only, who is at the Father's side, has made him known" (John 1:18). The Greek phrase translated "made him known" can in effect be transliterated into English as "exegeted him."

During His ministry the Lord Jesus made the same affirmation concerning His person. In response to His disciple Philip's request, "Lord, show us the Father and that will be enough for us" (John 14:8), Jesus responded with a note of sadness in His heart, if not His voice. "Don't you know me, Philip, even after I have been among you such a long time? Anyone who has seen me has seen the Father. How can you say, 'Show us the Father'?" (14:9). Philip's problem, despite his association with Jesus as a disciple from the beginning of Jesus' ministry (1:43), was that Jesus looked like any other person, such as one of the prophets of the Old Testament with divinely provided power to perform miracles. Philip recognized Jesus as the promised Messiah of the Old Testament (1:45), but he did not yet understand that Jesus is the God-Man, the union of deity and humanity in one person.

THE UNION OF GOD AND MAN IN ONE PERSON

The Council of Chalcedon (A.D. 451) provided a fairly lengthy and involved statement of the doctrine of the person of Christ incarnate. In brief it can be stated as the union of "full Deity and perfect humanity . . . without mixture, change, division, or separation in one Person forever."[1] This is called the hypostatic union. Like the doctrine of the Trinity, it "is one of the most intricate studies"[2] in the field of theology. This is because, again like the Trinity, the person of Jesus Christ is totally unique. Also, as in formulating the doctrine of the Trinity, we have only the testimony of Scripture in seeking to understand the doctrine of the person of Jesus Christ incarnate.

Formulating the doctrine of the incarnate person of Christ is complicated by Scripture that states the Incarnation involved a stepping down, a condescension. The apostle John wrote, "The Word became flesh and made his dwelling among us" (John 1:14). Speaking of Jesus' location and possibly His temporary position as well, the author of the epistle to the Hebrews stated that He "was made a little lower than the angels" (Heb. 2:9). If it involved position as well as location, it was only temporary, because elsewhere the author emphasized Jesus' superiority over the angels in His exaltation to "the right hand of the Majesty in heaven" (1:3; see vv. 4–13).

The difficulty in determining what the Incarnation involved in relation to Jesus' deity centers on the apostle Paul's statement that "being in very nature God, [He] did not consider equality with God something to be grasped, but made himself nothing" (Phil. 2:6–7). The Greek verb *kenoō*, rendered "emptied" in several translations (ASV, NASB), in transliteration provides the name for this step of condescension called "the kenosis." In another place Paul wrote concerning Christ, "though he was rich yet for your sakes he became poor" (2 Cor. 8:9). What this "emptying" or "becoming poor" meant is the crux of the problem.

The Full Deity of Jesus Christ

The kenosis did not involve the abandonment of any of the attributes or other elements of the nature of deity—something that God, being immutable, could not do. Otherwise Jesus would be less than God. In addition to Jesus' statement to Philip, He had stated earlier, "When a man believes in me, he does not believe in me only, but in the one who sent me. When he looks at me, he sees the one who sent me" (John 12:44–45). Even before that, in speaking to the Jews in the temple area at the Feast of Dedication, Jesus had declared, "I and the Father are one" (10:30). The neuter form of the Greek word translated "one" indicates that Jesus was speaking of a unity of nature with God the Father. The Jews picked up stones to stone Him for blasphemy, stating that "you, a mere man, claim to be God" (10:33). Still earlier Jesus had told the Jews, "I tell you the truth . . . before Abraham was born, I am" (8:58), applying to Himself the name by which God identified Himself to Moses and for Israel (Exod. 3:14). Here also the Jews recognized the significance of Jesus' claim and "picked up stones to stone him" (John 8:59).

If Jesus' claims to being God are not true, then either He was deluded or He was a deceiver; but His life, ministry, and teachings do not indicate Him to be either. Furthermore, other New Testament authors affirmed the deity of Jesus Christ. Before writing of Jesus' kenosis, Paul spoke of Jesus "being in very nature God" and His not considering "equality with God something to be grasped" (Phil. 2:6). Elsewhere Paul described Christ as "the image of the invisible God" (Col. 1:15; see 2 Cor. 4:4), and the author of the epistle to the Hebrews wrote that "in these last days he [God] has spoken to us by his Son" (Heb. 1:2), whom he described as "the radiance of God's glory and the exact representation of his being" (1:3). Paul called Jesus "God" (Rom. 5:2) and "our great God and Savior, Jesus Christ" (Titus 2:13).

Jesus exercised divine attributes. In His earthly life and ministry Jesus used numerous attributes possessed only by God. When Philip brought

Nathaniel to Jesus, the Lord said Nathanael was "a true Israelite, in whom there is nothing false" (John 1:47). This is more than human insight; it is divine omniscience (Ps. 139:1–6). When Nathaniel asked, "How do you know me?" Jesus answered, "I saw you while you were still under the fig tree before Philip called you" (John 1:48), thereby demonstrating divine omnipresence (Ps. 139:7–12). Jesus claimed divine eternality when He asked God the Father to "glorify me in your presence with the glory I had with you before the world began" (John 17:5). On several occasions Jesus demonstrated more than human knowledge of the thoughts of humans (Luke 6:8; 11:17; John 2:24–25); the most outstanding instance was when He told the Samaritan woman at the well of Sychar, "You are right when you say you have no husband. The fact is, you have had five husbands, and the man you now have is not your husband" (John 4:17–18). Jesus also demonstrated divine omnipotence in His control over the storm (Matt. 8:23–27; see Mark 4:36–39; Luke 8:23–24), His multiplication of the loaves and fish (Matt. 14:17–21; 15:34–38; 16:9–10; see Mark 6:38–44; 8:5–9), and His ability to restore life to the dead (Luke 7:12–15; Mark 5:22–24, 35–43; John 11:11–15, 21, 38–44).

Jesus exercised divine prerogatives. The exercise of divine prerogatives during His earthly ministry also demonstrates that Jesus did not lose any of His deity at His incarnation. One such prerogative is the forgiveness of sins, which Jesus exercised. On one occasion a paralyzed man in Capernaum was carried on a bed to Jesus by four friends. Unable to get to Jesus because of the crowd, they went to the roof, removed the tiles, and lowered their friend in front of Jesus (Mark 2:1–4; see Matt. 9:1–2, Luke 5:18-19). "When Jesus saw their faith, he said to the paralytic, 'Son, your sins are forgiven'" (Mark 2:5; see Matt. 9:2; Luke 5:20). Some of the "teachers of the law" mentally accused Jesus of blasphemy, correctly thinking to themselves, "Who can forgive sins but God alone?" (Mark 2:7; see Luke 5:21).

Knowing their thoughts (evidence of divine omniscience), Jesus said to them, "Which is easier; to say to the paralytic, 'Your sins are forgiven,' or to say, 'Get up, take your mat and walk'?" (Mark 2:9; see Matt. 9:5; Luke 5:23). Obviously it is easier to say "Your sins are forgiven," because who can tell outwardly whether they have been or not? Then Jesus said, "But that you may know that the Son of Man has authority on earth to forgive sins. . . . He said to the paralytic, 'I tell you, get up, take your mat and go home'" (Mark 2:10–11; see Matt. 9:6; Luke 5:24). Immediately the man "got up, took his mat and walked out in full view of them all" (Mark 2:12; see Matt. 9:7, Luke 5:25). By healing the paralytic Jesus demonstrated His divine prerogative to forgive sins.

On another occasion, when Jesus was eating dinner in a Pharisee's house, a "woman who had lived a sinful life in that town" (Luke 7:37) came and washed Jesus' "feet with her tears. Then she wiped them with her hair, kissed them and poured perfume on them" (7:38) as evidence of her repentance and faith. Jesus told her, "Your sins are forgiven. . . . Your faith has saved you; go in peace" (7:48, 50).

This sinful woman's ministry to Jesus was evidence of her faith in Him, for which she received forgiveness of her sins. But her washing His feet also expressed her worship of Him. The right to receive worship is another prerogative of the incarnate Lord Jesus. The Magi who came to Jerusalem looking for the "king of the Jews" said, "We have come to worship him" (Matt. 2:2). When they came to the house where Jesus was, "they bowed down and worshiped him" (2:11). After Jesus walked on the water, stilled the storm, and entered the boat, his disciples "worshiped him" (14:33). So did the man blind from birth whom Jesus healed (John 9:1, 38). It is not surprising that after Jesus' resurrection the women (Matt. 28:9) and the disciples (28:17) worshiped Him. And after His ascension the disciples worshiped the Lord as they returned to Jerusalem (Luke 24:52). Angels, too, worship Jesus, "the firstborn" (Heb. 1:6). He accepts worship because it is His prerogative as the incarnate Son of God.

A significant passage of Scripture that discusses Jesus' exercise of divine prerogatives is John 5:16–30. His basic affirmation to the Jews to whom He spoke was, "My Father is always at his work to this very day, and I, too, am working" (5:17). Later He said, "Whatever the Father does the Son also does" (5:19). Then Jesus claimed the authority to give "life to whom he is pleased to give it" (5:21), both physical life in resurrection and spiritual life in salvation. In addition Jesus said that God the Father "has entrusted all judgment to the Son, that all may honor the Son just as they honor the Father" (5:22–23). Jesus' authority over the resurrection of the dead and the judgment of everyone is stated more fully in verses 25–30.

The Perfect Humanity of Jesus Christ

The person of our Lord Jesus Christ involved the union of perfect humanity with full deity. This means that He was totally free of any taint of the Adamic sin nature. The angel Gabriel described the Virgin Mary's Holy-Spirit-conceived son as "the holy one" (Luke 1:35). This is not because Mary was "immaculate" as Roman Catholics believe. That only pushes the miracle back a generation and makes it more difficult to explain, because Mary was conceived normally by two parents with Adamic natures. Instead it was because God said to Mary, "The Holy Spirit will come upon you, and the power of the Most High will overshadow you" (1:35). Later in His ministry Jesus challenged the Jews who rejected His teaching; He asked, "Can any of you prove me guilty of sin?" (John 8:46).

Although He was free of sin by nature and by action, Jesus apparently lived a normal life. Luke reported that "the child grew and became strong; he was filled with wisdom, and the grace of God was upon him" (Luke 2:40). He displayed that wisdom when Joseph and Mary took Him to Jerusalem at the age of twelve and He was accidentally left behind. His parents found him "after three days . . . in the temple courts, sitting among the teachers, listening to them and asking them questions. Everyone who heard him was amazed at his understanding and his answers" (2:46–47). Luke wrote that he "was obedient to them. . . . And Jesus grew in wisdom and stature, and in favor with God and men" (2:51–52). What a shock it must have been to Mary when her next child showed the first evidence of his Adamic sin nature, which Jesus never displayed.

Jesus' human nature was perfect in the sense of His being free from sin. He was "without sin" (Heb. 4:15); He "had no sin" (2 Cor. 5:21), and "in him is no sin" (1 John 3:5). His human nature was also complete in that it included a soul and spirit and well as a body. As a result Jesus could feel the range of normal human emotions. He wept at the tomb of Lazarus (John 11:35) and the Jews said, "See how he loved him!" (11:36). He could feel righteous anger (Mark 3:5), which He displayed in driving the merchants and moneychangers out of the temple at His triumphal entry into Jerusalem (Matt. 21:12–13; see Mark 11:15–17; Luke 19:45–46). In the Garden of Gethsemane Jesus spoke of His soul being "overwhelmed with sorrow" (Matt. 26:38; see John 12:27).

Jesus learned the carpenter's trade from Joseph and was known as "the carpenter's son" (Matt. 13:55), and "the carpenter" (Mark 6:3). He became hungry (Matt. 4:2), thirsty (John 4:7; 19:28), and tired (4:6) like any human being. He was "tempted by the devil" (Matt. 4:1–11; see Mark 1:13; Luke 4:1–12). The author of the epistle to the Hebrews explained that "we have one who has been tempted in every way, just as we are—yet was without sin" (Heb. 4:15; see 2:18). By angelic instruction His parents named Him Jesus (Luke 1:31; 2:21; Matt. 1:21, 25), a meaningful name in Jewish history (Josh. 1:1), and Jesus delighted in calling Himself "the Son of Man" (Matt. 8:20, the first of eighty-nine times). Jesus truly lived as a Man among men.

THE RELATIONSHIP OF GOD AND MAN IN ONE PERSON

The Scriptures make it clear that Jesus is the union of full deity and perfect, complete humanity. Jesus is the God-Man. The Scriptures are not as clear, however, in delineating the relationship between the divine nature and the human nature in the person of Christ. They are clear that it is a hypostatic union, a union of natures to form one person. Jesus is the theanthropic person who feels and thinks and acts as one person. He is not a split personality with His divine and human natures in conflict. In Scripture Jesus never spoke of either His deity or His humanity as separate from Himself; He always spoke and acted as one person.

Errors concerning the Union

Nestorianism, named after Nestorius (died ca. A.D. 451), views Jesus as having a dual personality. This is only one of several errors advanced and rejected as the Christian church sought to understand the biblical teaching concerning the person of Jesus Christ. The earliest to be advanced is called "Docetism," derived from a transliteration of the Greek verb *dokeō*, which means "to seem." It taught that Jesus only seemed to be a man; His body was only an apparition. The apostle John refuted this view when he wrote, "Every spirit that acknowledges that Jesus Christ has come in the flesh is from God, but every spirit that does not acknowledge Jesus is not from God" (1 John 4:2–3). And John emphasized earlier, "That which was from the beginning, which we have heard, which we have seen with our eyes, which we have looked at and our hands have touched—this we proclaim concerning the Word of life" (1:1). Docetism is also mentioned in 2 John 7 ("deceivers, who do not acknowledge Jesus Christ as coming in the flesh") and refuted in Colossians 2:9 ("For in Christ all the fullness of the Deity lives in *bodily* form"). Ryrie accurately writes, "This heresy undermines not only the reality of the Incarnation but also the validity of the Atonement and bodily resurrection."[3]

Another early heresy concerning the person of Jesus is "Ebionism," named for a sect of Jewish Christians in the early centuries of the church. In effect it denied the virgin birth of Jesus, considering Him the natural son of Joseph and Mary. Ebionites taught that the eternal Christ was united with the human Jesus when John baptized Jesus. Some of them held that "the Christ" left Jesus on the cross, pointing to His cry, "My God, my God, why have you forsaken me?" (Matt. 27:46; Mark 15:34). According to this view Jesus died just as a man, not as the God-Man. Many Bible students believe 1 John 5:6–8 is a refutation of this heresy, which was advanced near the close of the apostolic era by Cerinthus and accepted by others. If Jesus was the natural son of Joseph and Mary, he was not "the holy one" (Luke 1:35), but received an Adamic sin nature from his parents. Furthermore, if He died as a man, His death could not be the infinite sacrifice for the sins of the world.

Still another heresy concerning the person of Christ in the early centuries of the church is Monarchianism. In an effort to preserve absolute monotheism in opposition to Trinitarianism, its adherents presented one of two points of view. The Adoptionist or Dynamic Monarchians "maintained that Jesus was God only in the sense that a power or influence from the Father rested upon His human person."[4] The Modalist Monarchians, also called Sabellians from Sabellius (third century A.D.), taught that "in the Godhead the only differentiation was a mere succession of modes or operations."[5] Modalism, however, is refuted by the separate presence of the three persons of the triune Godhead at Jesus' baptism by John the Baptist: "the Spirit of God [was] descending like a dove and resting on" Jesus (Matt. 3:16); God the Father in "a voice from heaven" identified Jesus as "my Son, whom I love" (3:17; see Mark 1:10–11; Luke 3:21–22). This group was also known as Patripassionists, because they taught that God the Father suffered and died as Jesus Christ, God the Son. A contemporary version of this error is the Jesus Only movement.

Arianism, named for its originator Arius (ca. A.D. 250–ca. 336), denied the eternality and full deity of the Word who became incarnate as Jesus Christ. Arianism taught that the Logos "was not eternal but was created by the Father from nothing as an instrument for the creation of the world; and that therefore he was not God by nature, but a changeable creature."[6] This heresy is promoted in our day by both the Jehovah's Witnesses and the Mormons (the Church of Jesus Christ of Latter-Day Saints). Charles Taze Russell, founder of the Watchtower Bible and Tract Society, which later became known as the Jehovah's Witnesses, described Jesus Christ as "the highest of all Jehovah's creation, so also he was the first, the direct creation of God, the 'only begotten,' and then, he, as Jehovah's power, and in his name, created all things—angels, principalities and powers, as well as the earthly creation."[7] The Mormon author James E. Talmadge affirmed the preexistence of Christ before His conception by Mary and birth in Bethlehem, but he taught that Jesus was not God, a member of the Trinity. Talmadge wrote, "He had lived with the Father as an unembodied spirit, the Firstborn of the Father's children."[8]

Another ancient error is called Eutychianism, named for its originator Eutychus (ca. A.D. 378–454). In opposition to Nestorianism, this view held that in the incarnate Christ deity and humanity were blended into one nature like the ingredients in a cake. As a result Jesus was not fully divine, and yet He was more than human; He had a theanthropic nature but was not the theanthropic person, the God-Man. This heresy is also known as Monophysitism, meaning "one nature," in the sense that He had *one* blended nature, not a divine nature and a human nature. A variation of this view is that, although Christ had two natures, He had only one will. This is known as Monothelitism. Even though Jesus could express His human will in the sense of wish or desire, as voiced in His prayer in the Garden of Gethsemane (Matt. 26:39, 42), His personal will in the sense of moral choice always followed the will of God the Father.

Since erroneous views of the relationship between the deity and humanity in the incarnate person of Christ arose before the close of the apostolic generation, it is understandable that the church of that time struggled to reach a position in accord with the biblical teaching. This was debated among church leaders and formulated in statements of church councils until the issue was more or less settled at the councils of Chalcedon (A.D. 451) and Constantinople (A.D. 680). Modern versions of these ancient heresies, however, underscore the need for constant vigilance to preserve the true biblical doctrine.

Describing the Union

The accounts of the incarnate life of Jesus in the Gospels help us draw accurate conclusions concerning the relationship between the divine and human natures in the person of Christ. A most important conclusion is that Jesus never used His deity to make life easier for Himself. When the devil challenged Him to prove He was the Son of God and satisfy His hunger by turning stones into bread (Matt. 4:3; Luke 4:3), something Jesus could do, He refused. His refusal was not just because it was the devil's challenge; it was also because He would not relieve His hunger through His divine powers. Similarly, Jesus never sent His disciples ahead of Him and then miraculously transported Himself there to meet them; He walked the dusty paths and grew weary along with the disciples. Before He walked on the water to meet His disciples in the boat after sending them ahead, He remained behind to pray (Matt. 14:23). He also wanted to teach impetuous and questioning Peter to keep looking to Jesus in faith instead of at the surrounding circumstances (14:15–33; see John 6:16–21).

On the other hand, the human nature of Jesus, although it was sinless at conception and birth (Luke 1:35), was subject to temptation and falling into sin in and of itself, just as the sinless human natures of Adam and Eve had been until they disobeyed God and sinned (Gen. 1:26–28: 2:15–18,

20–25; 3:6–13, 16–23). However, because Jesus' human nature was joined with His divine nature in one person, He not only did not sin when tempted by the devil or at any time later in His earthly life, but He could not sin. Theologically this is called the impeccability of Christ.

Some evangelical Christians, even though they state emphatically that Jesus never did sin, insist that He *could* have sinned. They base this belief in the peccability of Jesus on the reality and genuineness of His humanity. As stated by Charles Hodge, "If He was a true man, He must have been capable of sinning."[9] This argument, however, ignores the fact that the true humanity of Jesus was without a sin nature from conception (Luke 1:35). This view also overlooks the fact that His human nature was united with the divine nature of the eternal Son of God, the Word, into one Person. Though Jesus had a true human nature, He was more than a true man; He was the God-Man.

Christians who believe Jesus was capable of sinning (even though He never did sin) also base this belief on their understanding of temptation and the reality of Jesus' temptation. On this point Hodge wrote, "Temptation implies the possibility of sin. If from the constitution of his person it was impossible for Christ to sin, then his temptation was unreal and without effect, and He cannot sympathize with his people."[10]

However, this view misunderstands the meaning of temptation. The word in Hebrew, Greek, and English means primarily "to test" or "to prove by testing" and only secondarily "to solicit to do evil." The Old Testament states that Israel tempted "the LORD" (Exod. 17:2; Deut. 6:16; Mal. 3:15), and the New Testament speaks of tempting God (Acts 5:9; 15:10; 1 Cor. 10:9). Everyone would agree that God cannot sin because of "the constitution of his person," but God obviously can be and is tempted in the sense of being tested and proved by testing. But this is far different from Jesus having the ability to sin. A small tugboat attacking a huge ocean liner is unable to sink it; nonetheless it is still a real attack. In other words, for a temptation to be real, the one receiving the attack (Jesus) need not be susceptible to sin.

Also, when Hodge wrote that impeccability makes Christ's "temptation unreal and without effect," he misunderstood both the person of Christ and the character of His testing. After forty days of fasting, Jesus was hungry and humanly desirous of food to a degree few of us, if any, have ever known. Furthermore, through His divine nature He had the ability to turn stones into bread. However, the desires of Jesus' sinless human nature and the omnipotence of His divine nature were always controlled by the unified person and will of the God-Man, which always chose and acted in obedience to the will of God the Father (John 5:10; 8:59). Therefore it was impossible for Christ to sin.

Furthermore, He could and does "sympathize with his people" (Heb. 2:9–18; 4:14–16). This is true not only because Jesus experienced the normal human feelings and desires of His people apart from a sin nature, but also because His omniscience enables Him to know and sympathize with them.

We have already mentioned how Jesus displayed the omniscience, omnipotence, and omnipresence of God, but Scripture also reveals that He showed a lack of knowledge because of His human nature. As He walked along with Jairus, "a large crowd followed and pressed around him" (Mark 5:24). A woman who had suffered with a "bleeding for twelve years" (5:25) "touched His cloak" (5:27), thinking, "If I just touch his clothes, I will be healed" (5:28). Sensing that power had gone out from him, Jesus asked, "Who touched my clothes?" (5:30). Jesus may have known who she was and so He asked only to encourage the woman to respond, or His question may reflect ignorance from the standpoint of His human nature. When the healed woman came forward, Jesus told her, "Daughter, your faith has healed you. Go in peace and be freed from your suffering" (5:34). Later, in the Olivet Discourse, when speaking of the coming of the Son of Man (Matt. 24:27), Jesus said, "No one knows about that day or hour, not even the angels in heaven, not the Son, but only the Father" (Matt. 24:36; Mark 13:32; see Acts 1:7), again showing personal lack of knowledge in His human nature. This expression of the attributes of both His deity and His humanity in His single person is called the communion of attributes, the doctrine that "the attributes of both natures belong to the one Person without mixing the natures or dividing the Person."[11]

Our Lord Jesus' making "himself nothing"—perhaps more literally emptied himself—(Phil. 2:7, NASB), therefore, did not in any way constitute a laying aside of His deity or any of His divine attributes. It did involve voluntarily not using His divine attributes at times, as when He experienced human weariness and lack of knowledge, but Jesus always possessed a full divine nature. The glory of that divine nature was veiled, however, so that Christ Jesus was "made in human likeness" and was "found in appearance as a man" (2:7–8). At times that veil was removed, as when Jesus took Peter, James, and John "up a high mountain" where "he was transfigured before them. His face shone like the sun, and his clothes became as the light" (Matt. 17:1–2; Mark 9:2–3). His transfiguration explains why the apostle John could write, "We have seen his glory, the glory of the One and Only Son, who came from the Father, full of grace and truth" (John 1:14). Struck with the uniqueness of Jesus Christ, Napoleon Bonaparte wrote, "Everything in Christ astonishes me. His spirit overpowers men, and His will confounds me. Between Him and whoever else is in the world there is no comparison. He is truly a being by Himself."[12]

Phillips Brooks, a well-known nineteenth-century preacher, spoke of Jesus' humanity and deity in an interesting way:

> Here is a man who was born in an obscure village, the child of a peasant woman. He grew up in another obscure village. He worked in a carpenter's shop until he was thirty, and then for three years He was an itinerant preacher. He never wrote a book. He never held an office. He never owned a home. He never had a family. He never went to college. He never traveled two hundred miles from the place where He was born. He never did one of the things that usually accompany greatness. He had no credentials but Himself. He had nothing to do with the world except the power of His divine manhood. While still a young man, the tide of popular opinion turned against Him. He was turned over to His enemies. He was nailed on a cross between two thieves. His executioners gambled for the only piece of property He had on earth while He was dying—His coat. When He was dead, He was taken down and laid in a borrowed grave through the pity of a friend. And on the third day He arose from the dead. Nineteen centuries have come and gone, and today He is the centerpiece of the human race and the leader of the column of progress. I am far within the mark when I say that all the armies that ever marched, and all the navies that ever were built, and all the parliaments that ever sat, and all the kings

that ever reigned put together have not affected the life of man on earth as powerfully as has that One solitary life. The explanation? He is the Son of God, the risen Savior.[13]

Lewis Sperry Chafer made these comments about the incarnate Christ:

He was weary; yet He called the weary to Himself for rest. He was hungry; yet He was "the bread of life." He was thirsty; yet He was "the water of life." He was in agony; yet He healed all manner of sicknesses and soothed every pain. He "grew, and waxed strong in spirit"; yet He was from all eternity. He was tempted; yet He, as God, could not be tempted. He was self-limited in knowledge; yet He was the wisdom of God. He said, "My Father is greater than I" (with reference to His humiliation, being made for a little season lower than the angels); yet He also said, "He that hath seen me hath seen the Father," "I and my Father are one." He prayed, which is always human; yet He Himself answered prayer. He said, "This is your hour, and the power of darkness"; yet all power is given unto Him in heaven and in earth. He slept on a pillow in the boat; yet He arose and rebuked the storm. He was baptized, which was only a human act; yet at that time God declared Him to be His Son. He walked two long days' journey to Bethany; yet He knew the moment that Lazarus died. He wept at the tomb; yet He called the dead to arise. He confessed that He would be put to death; yet He had but a moment before received Peter's inspired declaration that He was the Christ, the Son of the living God. He said, "Whom do men say that I the Son of man am?"; yet John tells us, "He needed not that any should testify of man: for He knew what was in man." He was hungry; yet He could turn stones into bread. This He did not do; for had He done so, He would not have suffered as men suffer. He said, "My God, my God, why hast thou forsaken me?"; yet it was that very God to whom He cried who was "in Christ, reconciling the world unto himself." He dies; yet He is eternal life. He freely functioned in His earth-life within that which was perfectly human, and He as freely functioned in His earth-life within that which was perfectly divine. His earth-life, therefore, testifies as much to His humanity as to His Deity, and both of these revelations are equally true.[14]

Seven

THE EARTHLY LIFE AND MINISTRY
OF THE INCARNATE SON OF GOD

⸺◦⸺

HE LORD JESUS CHRIST was the union of the eternal Word, the second person of the triune Godhead, and perfect and complete humanity, from the moment of His conception by the Holy Spirit (Luke 1:35). Although it is not stated, Jesus, like John the Baptist, was undoubtedly "filled with the Holy Spirit even from birth" (1:15). As a result of His conception by the Holy Spirit, Jesus was "the holy one" (1:35), free from an Adamic sin nature, and His divine nature kept Him from committing sin even as a child and an adolescent.

Little is said in the Gospels, however, concerning Jesus' childhood and youth—simply His circumcision and naming on the eighth day (2:21), Mary's purification and Jesus' redemption by sacrifice as the firstborn thirty-three days later (Lev. 12; Luke 2:22–24), the flight and sojourn in Egypt until Herod's death (Matt. 2:13–15) and the return to Joseph and Mary's original hometown, Nazareth in Galilee, after Herod's death (2:19–23). The only other incident mentioned in the Gospels concerning Jesus' life before His baptism by John was the journey to Jerusalem with His parents for the Feast of the Passover when He was twelve years old (Luke 2:41–42). Jesus may have gone with them on previous trips, "but at twelve a Jewish boy became a 'son of the law' and began to observe the ordinances, putting on the phylacteries as a reminder."[1] This custom is now observed by Jews in the bar mitzvah at age thirteen. Luke wrote that "the child grew and became strong; he was filled with wisdom, and the grace of God was upon him" (2:40). And after the incident in Jerusalem He "went down to Nazareth with them and was obedient to them. . . . And Jesus grew in wisdom and stature, and in favor with God and men" (2:51–52).

Whether Jesus as a child was conscious of His divine nature is not stated, but perhaps He was not. It would seem that Jesus' response to Mary when His parents found Him in the temple—"Why were you searching for me? . . . Didn't you know I had to be in my Father's house?" (2:49)—was the first indication of His awareness of His unique relationship to God. The apocryphal and pseudopigraphal Gospels, however, are filled with fanciful tales of young Jesus restoring dead playmates to life, healing wounds and broken bones, and touching play birds made of clay and having them come to life and fly away. But the simplicity and sobriety of the true Gospels show their genuineness in contrast to these bizarre stories.

JESUS' BAPTISM

John the Baptist, son of Zechariah, began his ministry "in the fifteenth year of the reign of Tiberias Caesar . . . during the high priesthood of Annas and Caiaphas" (Luke 3:1–2). Because of the difficulty in correlating biblical events with the calendar in use today, the beginning of John's ministry is viewed as having occurred at some time between A.D. 27 and A.D. 29. After discussing all the options, one specialist in biblical chronology places it "sometime in A.D. 29,"[2] which would make John the Baptist thirty years old, the age when priests and Levites began their temple service (Num. 3:2–3, 22–23, 29–30). This would have been appropriate since John was qualified to be a priest (Luke 1:5). Since Jesus was slightly more than six months younger than John (1:36–38), His coming to John for baptism and the beginning of His ministry also took place when he was thirty years old.

The phrase introducing John's ministry is significant—"the word of God came to John" (3:2). Essentially the same phrase introduced the prophecies of Haggai (1:1), Zechariah (1:1), and Malachi (1:1), the three postexilic prophets before the four centuries of "silence" from God to Israel. It may be said, therefore, that John's ministry continued the Old Testament prophetic tradition. When John had been thrown into prison by Herod the tetrarch (Matt. 14:3–12; 11:1–2), Jesus said of John, "Then what did you go out to see? A prophet? Yes, I tell you, and more than a prophet" (11:9; Luke 7:26).

At the same time John the Baptist marked the transition to a new epoch in the outworking of God's eternal plan. Jesus continued to identify John as the forerunner of Israel's Messiah, quoting Malachi 3:1 (Matt. 11:10), and as "Elijah, who was to come" if he was accepted by the Jewish people (Matt. 11:14; 17:10–13; Mark 9:11–13; Luke 1:17; John 1:21–23; see Mal. 4:5). Jesus praised John, saying, "I tell you the truth: Among those born of women there has not risen anyone greater than John the Baptist" (Matt. 11:11; Luke 7:28).

The fact that John the Baptist's ministry was "in the Desert of Judea" (Matt. 3:1), "on the other side of the Jordan" (John 1:28) instead of in Jerusalem, shows that he stood apart from the established Jewish religious hierarchy of priests, scribes, Pharisees, and Sadducees. Efforts to identify John the Baptist with the Dead Sea sect because of his ministry in the Judean desert are groundless. He was described by the angel Gabriel to his father Zechariah as coming "in the spirit and power of Elijah" (Luke 1:17) and living as a Nazirite, not taking "wine or other fermented drink" (1:15; Num. 6:1–4), from birth. John dressed like Elijah (Matt. 3:4; 2 Kings 1:8), his diet was similar to Elijah's (Matt. 3:4; 1 Kings 17:3), and his location also was similar (Mark 1:4; Luke 3:3; 1 Kings 17:3), in fulfillment of the prophecy of Isaiah 40:3–5.

As the forerunner of God's Messiah, John's ministry was to call the Jewish people to "Repent, for the kingdom of heaven is near" (Matt. 3:2), "preaching a baptism of repentance for the forgiveness of sins" (Mark 1:4; Luke 3:3). He exhorted the various groups who came to him—tax collectors, soldiers, ordinary people—to "produce fruit in keeping with repentance" (Luke 3:8), giving each group specific instructions (3:10–14). He denounced the Pharisees and Sadducees who came to him as a "brood of vipers" (Matt. 3:7) and warned them not to rest in being descendants of Abraham without bearing the fruit of genuine repentance (3:8–9).

John the Baptist also proclaimed that "after me will come one who is more powerful than I, whose sandals I am not fit to carry. He will baptize you with the Holy Spirit and with fire" (Matt. 3:11; Mark 1:7; Luke 3:16; John 1:15, 26, 30). John then explained that "the reason I came baptizing with water was that he might be revealed to Israel" (1:31), which was accomplished when Jesus was baptized by John. Jesus' baptism "with fire" probably refers to His judgment to come, in which He will purge, as if by fire, unbelievers from His kingdom (see Matt. 3:12). The apostle John wrote that John the Baptist also proclaimed Jesus as "the Lamb of God, who takes away the sin of the world!" (John 1:29; see v. 36). John recognized and accepted his part in God's program, telling his disciples when they complained about Jesus' growing popularity (3:26), "You yourselves can testify that I said, 'I am not the Christ but am sent ahead of him.'. . . . He must become greater; I must become less" (3:28, 30).

As already noted, Jesus was approximately six months younger than John the Baptist (Luke 1:36); therefore He was thirty years old when He was baptized by John. When Jesus came to him, John demurred, saying, "I need to be baptized by you, and do you come to me?" (Matt. 3:14). Jesus responded, "Let it be so now; it is proper for us to do this to fulfill all righteousness" (3:15). Bible students have puzzled over His meaning. Jesus did not need to repent of sin, as did others whom John baptized. But He did need to identify with sinners for whom He would provide the redemptive sacrifice in His death. In a sense His baptism by John also constituted His induction into His messianic office and ministry, since it resulted in His anointing by the Holy Spirit and His approval by God the Father as "he went up out of the water" (3:16).

Although Jesus' anointing was of a more exalted kind, it followed the pattern of Israel's custom of anointing kings (1 Sam. 10:1; 1 Kings 1:34–35, 38–39; 19:16; 2 Kings 9:6; 11:12), priests (Exod. 28:41; 29:7; 30:30–33; 40:13–15), and on at least one occasion (and possibly more) prophets (1 Kings 19:16; see 1 Chron. 16:22; Ps. 105:15). This anointing marked their appointment to and/or induction into office.

Although Jesus most likely was filled with the Holy Spirit from birth as was John the Baptist (Luke 1:15), the descent of the Spirit on Him "as a dove" (John 1:32, 33; see Matt. 3:16; Mark 1:10; Luke 3:21) marked His identity as the promised Messiah and His induction into that office and ministry. This was also confirmed by an audible voice from heaven that said, "This is my Son, whom I love; with him I am well pleased" (Matt. 3:17; see Mark 1:11; Luke 3:22). God the Father repeated the same words of approval of Jesus at His transfiguration (Matt. 17:5; Mark 9:7; Luke 9:35). As stated before, at Jesus' baptism all three persons of the Godhead were present: Jesus, the incarnate Son of God, God the Holy Spirit, and God the Father.

JESUS' MESSAGE AND MINISTRY AS GOD'S PROMISED MESSIAH

Although the eternal Word of God became incarnate as Jesus, to be "the Lamb of God, who takes away the sin of the world!" (John 1:29), He also came as the Messiah for God's people Israel, as promised in the Old Testament. This is stated in Gabriel's announcement to Mary (Luke 1:32–33) and in the angel's proclamation to the shepherds (2:11). To prepare the Jewish people for their Messiah was the point of John the Baptist's message and ministry. As a result, from the beginning of Jesus' earthly ministry to His crucifixion an important part of Jesus' message and ministry was presenting Himself to the Jewish people as their promised Messiah.

At the beginning of His ministry Jesus' message was the same as John's—"Repent, for the kingdom of heaven is at hand" (Matt. 4:17; see 3:2; Mark 1:14–15). As Jesus traveled "in all Galilee" He proclaimed "the good news of the kingdom" (Matt. 4:23; 9:35). When He returned to Nazareth, Jesus read in the synagogue the part of a messianic prophecy from Isaiah that applied to His earthly ministry (Luke 4:18–19; see Isa. 61:1–2a), and He said, "Today this scripture is fulfilled in your hearing" (Luke 4:21). Although Jesus did not "proclaim freedom to the prisoners" literally in His ministry on earth in His first coming, He did in the sense of providing freedom from physical bondage to disease (e.g., 5:12–13) and disability (John 5:3–8) and from mental bondage (Luke 8:2–3, 27–33, 35). In addition He certainly did "preach good news to the poor . . . recovery of sight to the blind" (e.g., John 9:1–7), released "the oppressed," and proclaimed "the year of the Lord's favor." Jesus told the twelve apostles,

"'Do not go among the Gentiles or enter any town of the Samaritans. Go rather to the lost sheep of Israel. As you go, preach this message: 'The kingdom of heaven is near'" (Matt. 10:5–7; see Luke 9:21).

When John the Baptist languished in Herod the tetrarch's prison and Jesus did nothing to set him free, he began to question if Jesus was the promised Messiah. So John sent two of his disciples to Jesus asking, "Are you the one who was to come, or should we expect someone else?" (Luke 7:19; Matt. 11:3). Jesus told them to tell John that they had seen the blind receive their sight, the lame walk, lepers cured, the deaf healed, and the dead raised, and that the good news was being preached to the poor (Luke 7:22; Matt. 11:4–5). At the close of His earthly ministry in His triumphal entry into Jerusalem Jesus was clearly presenting Himself to the Jewish people as their Messiah in fulfillment of Old Testament prophecies (Matt. 21:1–11; Mark 11:1–11; Luke 19:28–40; John 12:12–16; see Isa. 62:11; Zech. 9:9).

It is important to recognize, however, that Jesus' offer of Himself as the Messiah was rejected by both the Jewish leaders and the people. Before "the chief priests and the whole Sanhedrin" (Mark 14:55) Jesus responded "I am" to the high priest's question, "Are you the Christ, the Son of the Blessed One?" (14:61–62; see Matt. 26:63–64; Luke 22:66–70). But they condemned Him for blasphemy instead of accepting His testimony (Mark 14:63–64; see Matt. 26:65–66). Likewise, when "Pilate asked Jesus, 'Are you the king of the Jews?'" Jesus responded, "'Yes, it is as you say'" (Luke 23:3; John 18:33–37).

When Pilate presented Jesus to the Jewish leaders and people as "Christ" (Matt. 27:22) and "the king of the Jews" (Mark 15:12; John 19:14), they shouted, "Take him away! Take him away! Crucify him" (19:15; see Matt. 27:22–23; Mark 15:12–13). When Pilate asked the Jews, "Shall I crucify your king?" the chief priests answered, "We have no king but Caesar" (John 19:15). Similarly, when Pilate told the Jews that Jesus' death would be their responsibility, "All the people answered, 'Let his blood be on us and on our children'" (Matt. 27:25). This rejection of Jesus as Messiah and King by the Jewish leaders and people has implications for dispensationalism, which are discussed in chapter 8.

Jesus' earthly message and ministry identified Him as a prophet as well as the promised Messiah. Jesus spoke of Himself as a prophet when

He alluded to His death in Jerusalem by saying, "It cannot be that a prophet perish out of Jerusalem" (Luke 13:33, KJV). He was often called a prophet by others because of His miracles (Mark 6:15; Luke 7:16; John 6:14; 9:17), His teaching (7:40), and His knowledge of individuals' lives (4:19). His followers called Him "Jesus the prophet, from Nazareth in Galilee" (Matt. 21:11; see v. 46; Luke 24:19).

Jesus' prophetic ministry involved both His preaching and teaching and also His predictions of His death and resurrection (John 2:19, 21–22; Matt. 16:21), of the destruction of the temple (Matt. 24:2), and of the sign of His coming and "of the end of the age" (24:3), as well as other events. A great example of His teaching is the Sermon on the Mount (Matt. 5–7), which has been called "The Manifesto of the King." Lewis Sperry Chafer says that it "was given . . . as a feature of the kingdom proclamation which first occupied the ministry of Christ on earth. It constituted the authoritative edict of the King relative to the character of the kingdom, its requirements, and the conditions of admission into it."[3] Both John the Baptist and Jesus were preaching, "Repent, for the kingdom of heaven is near" (3:2; 4:17), so that, although the Sermon on the Mount had both immediate application to Jesus' audience and to readers today, it ultimately relates to the millennial kingdom of righteousness and peace. When Jesus finished it, "the crowds were amazed at his teaching, because he taught as one who had authority [which He did], and not as their teachers of the law" (7:28–29; see 13:54; 22:33; Mark 1:22; 6:2; 11:18; Luke 4:32; John 7:46).

JESUS' AUTHENTICATION AS MESSIAH BY HIS MIRACLES

Much of Jesus' ministry was occupied in the performance of a wide range of miracles. The Gospels record a total of thirty-five separate miracles.[4] The first one was the turning of water into wine, recorded in John 2:1–10. John wrote that His miracles were "miraculous signs" (2:11) or just "signs" (NKJV, ASV). In the New Testament four Greek nouns are used, all translated "miracle" in English at times. On the basis of those words Henry Thiessen defines a miracle as "a unique and extraordinary event awakening wonder (*teras*), wrought by divine power (*dynamis*), accomplishing some practical and benevolent work (*ergon*), and authenticating a messenger and his message as from God (*sēmeion*)."[5] This definition certainly applies to the miracles of Christ, especially His authentication as God's promised Messiah.

Jesus' miracles identified Him as the Christ in accord with Old Testament prophecies (Isa. 35:5–6; 61:1). Jesus never performed miracles for His own gratification (Matt. 4:2–4) or exaltation (4:5–7), but for the benefit of others (e.g., feeding the five thousand [14:14–21] and the four thousand [15:32–39]) or as a testimony to others concerning His identity as God's Messiah, the Son of God (e.g., stilling a storm [8:23–27] and "walking on the lake" [14:25–33]). Jesus' miracles relieved physical suffering and hardship of various kinds (e.g., 8:2–4; 9:2–8; 12:9–13), even restoring life to the dead (9:18–19, 23–25; Luke 7:11–15; John 11:11–14, 17–44). He exorcised demons (Matt. 8:28–33; 9:32–33; 12:22; 17:14–18; Mark 1:21–28). Also He performed miracles pertaining to nature, such as an abundance of fish (Luke 5:1–11; John 21:1–11), locating the tribute money (Matt. 17:24–27), and causing a fruitless fig tree to wither (21:18–19). Jesus undoubtedly performed many other miracles as well, because on numerous occasions Matthew wrote of Jesus "healing every disease and sickness among the people" (4:23–24; see 8:16; 9:35; 11:21, 23; 12:15; 14:14, 36; 15:30–31; 19:2; 21:14) and the apostle John wrote, "Jesus did many other things as well" (John 21:25), which undoubtedly included miracles.

Since Jesus was primarily presenting Himself to the Jewish people as God's promised Messiah in His earthly life and ministry, He traveled mainly between Galilee and Judea. On some of His trips between Galilee and Jerusalem He avoided Samaria, where people of mixed ancestry lived, by going around it through Decapolis. Jesus also instructed the twelve apostles when He sent them out, "Do not go among the Gentiles or enter any town of the Samaritans. Go rather to the lost sheep of Israel" (Matt. 10:5–6). On one occasion when "Jesus withdrew to the region of Tyre and Sidon" (15:21), a woman with a demon-possessed daughter came to Him asking for His help (15:22, 25). Matthew identified her as a "Canaanite woman" and Mark stated she "was a Greek, born in Syrian Phoenicia" (Mark 7:26). Emphasizing His messianic ministry, Jesus said, "I am sent only to the lost sheep of Israel" (Matt. 15:24). In response to her plea,

"Lord, help me!" (15:25), Jesus said, "It is not right to take the children's bread and toss it to their dogs" (15:26), still emphasizing His messianic ministry to the Jewish people and undoubtedly also testing the genuineness of the woman's faith. "Yes, Lord," the woman replied, "but even the dogs eat the crumbs that fall from their masters' table" (15:27). "Then Jesus answered, 'Woman, you have great faith! Your request is granted.' And her daughter was healed from that very hour" (15:28).

It is important to point out that the Lord Jesus recognized the humanity-wide outreach of His messianic mission (see Isa. 42:6–7; 49:6) and that He ministered to Gentiles and Samaritans on numerous occasions. The centurion whose highly valued servant was sick was undoubtedly a Gentile, probably a Roman (Luke 7:2), a conclusion drawn from the fact that he "sent some of the elders of the Jews" to Jesus to seek help (7:3). They told Jesus, "This man deserves to have you do this, because he loves our nation and has built our synagogue" (7:4–5). When the man sent word that he trusted Jesus simply to say the word and his servant would be healed, Jesus told "the crowd following him . . . 'I have not found such great faith even in Israel'" (7:9), and he healed the servant.

When He rebuked the Jewish people for their failure to respond to His miracles and accept Him as their Messiah, Jesus referred to the ministry of the Old Testament prophets to Gentiles as examples of God's humanity-wide working. He reminded the people in Nazareth that Elijah ministered "to a widow in Zarephath, in the region of Sidon" (4:26) and Elisha healed "Naaman the Syrian" of leprosy (4:27). When Jesus reproached the people in the cities of Galilee for their failure to repent, He told them, "If the miracles that were performed in you had been performed in Tyre and Sidon, they would have repented long ago in sackcloth and ashes" (Matt. 11:21), and "if the miracles that were performed in you had been performed in Sodom, it would have remained to this day" (11:23). These statements are a display of Jesus' divine omniscience.

Jesus also ministered to Samaritans even though "Jews do not associate with Samaritans" (John 4:9). The animosity between these peoples goes back to the people of the land—ancestors of the Samaritans—who hindered the Jews' efforts to rebuild Jerusalem after their return from exile in Babylon (Ezra 4). On one occasion when Jesus and His disciples were passing through Samaria on the way to Jerusalem, the people in the village where He sent His disciples to make arrangements "did not welcome him, because He was heading for Jerusalem" (Luke 9:53). This animosity explains the Samaritan woman's surprise at the well of Sychar when Jesus asked, "Will you give me a drink?" (John 4:7). The conversation resulted in Jesus' spiritual ministry to her, His disclosure that He is the Messiah (4:25–26), and His spiritual ministry to many of the Samaritans of Sychar (4:29–30, 39–41).

Amazingly, Jesus held Samaritans up to the Jewish people as examples of gratitude and helpfulness. When Jesus healed ten lepers in a village "along the border between Samaria and Galilee" (Luke 17:11), the one who "came back, praising God . . . and [who] threw himself at Jesus' feet and thanked him . . . was a Samaritan" (17:15–16). Whether the parable of the Good Samaritan is a report of an actual incident or not, the Samaritan, not the priest or the Levite, was the one who had compassion on the victim of the robbers (10:30–37). When the Greeks who were Jewish proselytes at the Passover in Jerusalem came to Philip saying, "Sir, we wish to see Jesus" (John 12:20–21), Jesus rejoiced in the humanity-wide provision of redemption from sin and salvation to be accomplished through His death. He said, "But I, when I am lifted up from the earth"—a reference to His crucifixion, not His ascension—"will draw all men to myself" (12:32). He did not mean by this that everyone would be saved, but that all kinds of people would come to Him, including Greek Gentiles who were present then (12:20). He draws people to Himself without discrimination, without regard for their nationality or ethnic background.[6] As Jesus told Nicodemus, "God so loved the world that he gave his one and only Son, that whoever believes in him shall not perish but have eternal life" (3:16). The apostle John wrote, "Yet to all who received him, to those who believed in his name, he gave the right to become children of God" (1:12).

JESUS' MISSION TO DIE ON THE CROSS
AS THE REDEMPTIVE SACRIFICE

Not only was the Incarnation of the eternal Word a part of the triune Godhead's eternal plan but so also was His substitutionary redemptive sacrifice on the cross to provide salvation and eternal life for all who believe in Him. In the Book of the Revelation He is called "the Lamb that was slain from the creation of the world" (Rev.13:8). The epistle to the Hebrews states, "When Christ came into the world, he said: 'Sacrifice and offering you did not desire, but a body you prepared for me. . . . Then I said, . . . I have come to do your will, O God'" (Heb. 10:5, 7). A veiled prophecy of Jesus' death was made to Mary when Simeon told her, "A sword will pierce your own soul" (Luke 2:35). In addition, whether he was aware of its full significance or not, John the Baptist identified Jesus at His baptism as "the Lamb of God, who takes away the sin of the world!" (John 1:29–36).

A question to be considered, however, is, When was the incarnate Christ conscious that He would die on the cross as God's redemptive sacrifice for sin? Some theologians say He was not aware of His coming sacrificial death. However, He apparently lived with this consciousness from very early in His ministry. When He drove the merchants and moneychangers out of the temple at the Feast of Passover after turning the water into wine, "the Jews demanded of him, 'What miraculous sign can you show us to prove your authority to do all this?'" (John 2:18). Jesus' enigmatic response was, "Destroy this temple, and I will raise it again in three days" (2:19). John explained that "the temple he had spoken of was his body. After he was raised from the dead, his disciples recalled what he had said. Then they believed the Scripture and the words that Jesus had spoken" (2:21–22).

Jesus' interview with Nicodemus apparently occurred on that same trip to Jerusalem. He told Nicodemus, "Just as Moses lifted up the snake in the desert, so the Son of Man must be lifted up, that everyone who believes in him may have eternal life" (3:14). From these two statements it is obvious that our Lord was conscious both of the manner of His death and its significance and of His resurrection.

Jesus began to share the necessity of His death and the fact of His resurrection with His disciples after Peter declared—undoubtedly speaking for the group—"You are the Christ, the Son of the living God" (Matt. 16:16; Mark 8:29; Luke 9:20; see John 11:27). Jesus told them that "he must go to Jerusalem and suffer many things at the hands of the elders, chief priests and teachers of the law, and that he must be killed and on the third day be raised to life" (Matt. 16:21; Mark 8:31; Luke 9:22). Peter, again probably speaking for the group, "took him aside and began to rebuke him," saying, "Never, Lord! . . . This shall never happen to you" (Matt. 16:22). With their recognition of Jesus as the Messiah, Peter and the other disciples were anticipating the restoration of the kingdom to Israel and the reestablishment of His reign on David's throne, not the Messiah's rejection and death as the Suffering Servant of God (Isa. 52:13–53:12).

Somewhat earlier than His revelation to the apostles about His upcoming death and resurrection Jesus had responded to a request from "some of the Pharisees and teachers of the law" for "a miraculous sign" (Matt. 12:38; 16:1; Mark 8:11; Luke 11:16), by saying, "A wicked and adulterous generation asks for a miraculous sign! But none will be given it except the sign of the prophet Jonah. For as Jonah was three days and three nights in the belly of a huge fish, so the Son of Man will be three days and three nights in the heart of the earth" (Matt. 12:39-40; 16:4; Mark 8:12; Luke 11:29–30, 32). This not only predicted His death somewhat enigmatically but also confirmed His acceptance of the factual occurrence of the prophet Jonah's miraculous experience.

After His disclosure of the necessity of His death and resurrection to His apostles, "Jesus resolutely set out for Jerusalem" (Luke 9:51). Interestingly, Luke related this not to Jesus' awareness of His approaching death but to His glorification: "As the time approached for him to be taken up to heaven." Jesus' settled resolve to obey God's will, even though it involved death by crucifixion, is illustrated and underscored by what immediately follows. When one prospective disciple wanted first to go back and say goodbye to his family, Jesus responded, "No one who puts his hand to the plow and looks back is fit for service in the kingdom of God" (9:62). On this final journey to Jerusalem Jesus again told His apostles the trip would end in His arrest, suffering, death, and resurrection (18:31–34).

Despite His commitment to fulfill God's will as the sinless incarnate Son of God, Jesus' shrinking back from being made "sin for us " (2 Cor. 5:21; see Gal. 3:13) is understandable. This reluctance is displayed in Jesus' agonizing prayer in the Garden of Gethsemane the night of His arrest. When He asked Peter, James, and John to watch while He went on to pray,

He said, "My soul is overwhelmed with sorrow to the point of death" (Matt. 26:38; Mark 14:34). Then Jesus went "a little farther . . . fell with his face to the ground and prayed, 'My Father, if it be possible, may this cup be taken from me. Yet not as I will, but as you will'" (Matt. 26:39; Mark 14:35–36; Luke 22:41–42). In the Old Testament a "cup" sometimes symbolized wrath (Jer. 25:15), and so Jesus was aware that His coming death meant He would bear the wrath of God the Father against sin. Though Christ had no sin (2 Cor. 5:21), He bore the sins of the world on Himself (1 Pet. 2:24). Thus He was made "a curse for us" because of His being hanged on a tree (Gal. 3:13).

Luke reported that "an angel from heaven appeared to him and strengthened him. And being in anguish, he prayed more earnestly, and his sweat was like drops of blood falling to the ground" (Luke 22:43–44). After finding the disciples sleeping, Jesus left again and prayed, "My Father, if it is not possible for this cup to be taken away unless I drink it, may your will be done" (Matt. 26:42; Mark 14:36). Finding the disciples sleeping again, Jesus went a third time, repeating the same prayer (Matt. 26:44), which reveals the depths of His agony (see Heb. 5:7–8).

At Jesus' arrest, one of His disciples "reached for his sword, drew it out and struck the servant of the high priest, cutting off his ear" (Matt. 26:51). John revealed that this disciple was Simon Peter (John 18:10). Jesus then made two interesting statements. First He told Peter, "Do you think I cannot call on my Father, and he will at once put at my disposal more than twelve legions of angels? But how then would the Scriptures be fulfilled that say it must happen this way?" (Matt. 26:53–54). This shows His complete control of the situation. Then He also said, "Shall I not drink the cup the Father has given me?" (John 18:11), showing His complete submission to God's will. To the same point, when Pilate told Jesus, "Don't you realize I have power either to free you or to crucify you?" Jesus responded, "You would have no power over me if it were not given to you from above" (19:10–11).

The Jewish Sanhedrin condemned Jesus as "worthy of death" for what they believed was blasphemy (Matt. 26:65–67; Mark 14:63–64; Luke 22:70–71). They took Him to Pilate, the Roman governor, because, as they said, "we have no right to execute anyone" . . . so that the words Jesus had spoken indicating the kind of death he was going to die would be fulfilled" (John 18:31–32). Pilate told the Jews that Jesus' death was their responsibility (Matt. 27:24), to which they responded, "Let his blood be on us and on our children" (27:25). But along with the Jews, the Roman government and the Gentiles were also responsible for rejecting and crucifying Jesus.

The spiritual atmosphere of Jesus' crucifixion is seen in the fact that "from the sixth hour until the ninth hour darkness came over all the land" (27:45; Mark 15:33; Luke 23:44). "About the ninth hour Jesus cried out in a loud voice . . . 'My God, my God, why have you forsaken me'?" (Matt. 27:46; Mark 15:34). It was at this point, as Jesus bore the sin of the world, that God, the Judge of sin, turned away from Jesus Christ, His incarnate Son, the Sin-bearer, as far as the personal consciousness of Jesus was concerned. Jesus said, "My God, my God," not "my Father, my Father," because God the Father did not forsake His only Son. There never was, nor could there be, separation between the persons of the Godhead. Then "Jesus called out in a loud voice, 'Father, into your hands I commit my spirit'" (Luke 23:46). John recorded that Jesus said, "It is finished" (John 19:30), signifying the completion of His propitiatory, redemptive sacrifice for sin. "With that," John continued, Jesus "bowed his head and gave up his spirit" (19:30; Matt. 27:50).

By using B.C. and A.D. our calendars count the years from the incarnation of the eternal Word as Jesus Christ, but in a very significant sense His death, not his birth, is the fulcrum of cosmic history. One indication of that fact is that "at that moment the curtain of the temple was torn in two from top to bottom" (Matt. 27:51; Mark 15:38; Luke 23:45). This was the work of God to signify the end of the Mosaic Covenant and system with its countless offerings and sacrifices, because the one final, perfect sacrifice had now been made (see Heb. 7:26–28; 9:11–10:4, 9–12). The Jewish sacrifices undoubtedly continued until the destruction of the temple under the Roman general Titus in A.D. 70, and Jewish worship continues today, but the death of Jesus marked the end of the Mosaic Covenant and the establishment of the New Covenant based on the finished work of Christ.

The death of Jesus also marked the fulfillment of God's prophecy to the serpent in the Garden of Eden that he, that is, the devil, would strike the heel of the offspring of the woman (Gen. 3:15). At Jesus' death Satan and his forces of evil were seemingly victorious. In truth, however, the very opposite took place; Jesus Christ's death, followed as it was by His resurrection, marked Satan's defeat. Jesus shared in "humanity so that by his death he might destroy him who holds the power of death—that is, the devil" (Heb. 2:14; see John 12:31; 1 John 3:8). Satan has not yet been removed from this world, but he is a defeated foe, his final destiny is certain (Rev. 20:1–3, 7–10), and Christians can enjoy victory over him and his evil hosts (Eph. 6:10–17; 1 Pet. 5:8–9; 1 John 4:4).

The cross of Jesus Christ, God's incarnate Son, was God the Father's exclamation point—His declaration "It is finished" for the salvation of those who believe in Him.

Part 3

THE GLORIFIED
CHRIST OF GOD

Eight

CHRIST'S ASCENSION TO THE
RIGHT HAND OF GOD THE FATHER

———◦◉◦———

WHEN THE APOSTLE PAUL presented the Lord Jesus Christ as the example for the Christian's proper spiritual attitude, he moved directly from Jesus' humility and obedience to God in suffering and death ("he humbled himself and became obedient to death—even death on a cross!") to the height of His glorification ("Therefore God exalted him to the highest place and gave him the name that is above every name," Phil. 2:8–9). Our Lord did the same thing in His high priestly prayer when He asked, "Father, the time has come. Glorify your Son, that your Son may glorify you. . . . I have brought you glory on earth by completing the work you gave me to do. And now, Father, glorify me in your presence with the glory I had with you before the world began" (John 17:1, 4–5). Luke related Jesus' heading for Jerusalem to suffer and die to "the time . . . for him to be taken up to heaven" (Luke 9:51).

In this regard Jesus' encounter with Mary Magdala early on the morning of His resurrection is interesting. When Mary realized it was Jesus and not the gardener, she apparently embraced Him, because Jesus told her, "Do not hold on to me, for I have not yet returned to the Father" (John 20:17). Some writers teach that the resurrected Jesus was about to ascend to heaven at that moment to present His blood in the Most Holy Place of the heavenly tabernacle (Heb. 9:11–14, 23–26). They conclude that Mary's embrace would have contaminated Him and His blood and rendered His presentation of His blood in heaven ineffective. However, what Jesus was really telling Mary was that, though He appeared to her to be the same as He was before His crucifixion, He was a different person with an immortal body whose proper residence was in heaven at the right hand of God. From the divine perspective, moving from the tomb to the throne was one giant step. Jesus' resurrection appearances and ministry were only a temporary "stop-off" on His way to His rightful glorification.

GLORIFIED IN RESURRECTION

Since exaltation to the right hand of God the Father was the goal of Christ's glorification, why did He spend forty days (Acts 1:3) in resurrection appearances and ministry to His disciples? First, it gave them "many convincing proofs that he was alive" (1:3). The Jewish leaders bribed the soldiers who had guarded Jesus' tomb to spread the story that "His disciples came during the night and stole him away while we were asleep" (Matt. 28:13). While the disciples would know this was not true, without resurrection appearances by Jesus they would not know what had happened with His body.

Second, Jesus' disciples needed instruction from Jesus' appearances to prepare them for their ministry after His ascension. Luke wrote that during His resurrection ministry Jesus spoke to His disciples "about the kingdom of God" (Acts 1:3). He also told them, "Do not leave Jerusalem, but wait for the gift my Father promised, which you have heard me speak about. For John baptized with water, but in a few days you will be baptized with the Holy Spirit" (1:4–5).

During Jesus' ministry before His death, the disciples were so preoccupied with His identity as the Messiah and the prospect of the restoration of the kingdom to Israel that they could not grasp His revelation to them about His approaching death and resurrection (Matt. 16:22; Mark 8:31–32; 9:31–32; Luke 9:21–22, 44–45). The two disciples to whom Jesus appeared on the road to Emmaus illustrate this situation. Their faces were downcast (Luke 24:17), and they told Jesus, "We had hoped that he was the one who was going to redeem Israel" (24:21). Even after His resurrection, when the disciples met with the resurrected Jesus, the Eleven asked, "Lord, are you at this time going to restore the kingdom to Israel?" (Acts 1:6). This question shows that they expected the kingdom would come when the Holy Spirit came. Obviously Christ had a vital resurrection ministry in teaching His disciples, including His special instructions to Simon Peter (John 21:15–19) and His giving of the Great Commission to the eleven disciples (Matt. 28:18–20; see Acts 1:8).

The Lord's Immortal Body

It is important to remember that the Lord Jesus was the first person to experience resurrection and to occupy an immortal body. The apostle Paul affirmed, "Christ has indeed been raised from the dead, the firstfruits of those who have fallen asleep" (1 Cor. 15:20), and he revealed that "in Christ all will be made alive. But each in his own turn: Christ, the firstfruits" (15:22–23). All those whom He had restored to life, including Lazarus, who had been in the tomb "four days" (John 11:39), were restored to physical life, not resurrected to immortality. Presumably they died again. Apparently this also applies to those who "were raised to life" in conjunction with the earthquake that occurred when Jesus died on Mount Calvary (Matt. 27:52). However, since "after Jesus' resurrection they went into the holy city and appeared to many people" (27:53), their being "raised to life" may have occurred after Jesus' resurrection and was a true resurrection. If this is true, they were taken to heaven at the time of Jesus' ascension.

In his sermon on the Day of Pentecost Peter said, "God raised him [Jesus] from the dead, freeing him from the agony of death, because it was impossible for death to keep its hold on him" (Acts 2:24). Then he quoted from a psalm of David: "My body also will live in hope, because you will not abandon me to the grave, nor will you let your Holy One see decay" (2:26–27; Ps. 16:9–10). Peter pointed out that David was not speaking of himself, because he "died and was buried, and his tomb is here to this day" (Acts 2:29). Instead he was speaking prophetically "of the resurrection of the Christ, that he was not abandoned to the grave, nor did his body see decay. God has raised this Jesus to life, and we are all witnesses of the fact" (2:31–32).

The point is that the same body of Jesus that was physically abused (Isa. 52:14), nailed to the cross, and placed in Joseph of Arimathea's "own new tomb" (Matt. 27:60; see Luke 23:53; John 19:41) was resurrected to eternal life immortal and imperishable. The characteristics of His resurrection body are the pattern of the resurrection bodies believers will receive either when our Lord comes in the air to translate His body, the church, to heaven (1 Thess. 4:13–18) or when He returns to earth to establish His kingdom (Rev. 20:4–6). Paul explained to the Corinthians, "So will it be with the resurrection of the dead. The body that is sown is perishable, it is raised imperishable; it is sown in dishonor, it is raised in glory; it is sown in weakness, it is raised in power; it is sown a natural body, it is raised a spiritual body.... And just as we have borne the likeness of the earthly man, so shall we bear the likeness of the man from heaven" (1 Cor. 15:42–44, 49).

The fact that Jesus' resurrection body had identity with the body that was placed in the tomb is substantiated by His inviting the ones gathered the evening of His resurrection to look at "His hands and feet" (Luke 24:39–40). Obviously His body still bore the nail holes of His crucifixion. Thomas, who was not present then, declared, "Unless I see the nail marks in his hands and put my finger where the nails were, and put my hand in his side, I will not believe it" (John 20:25). When Jesus appeared to the group "a week later . . . and Thomas was with them" (20:26), He told Thomas, "Put your finger here; see my hands. Reach out your hand and put it into my side" (20:27). Jesus also had told His disciples earlier, "Touch me and see; a ghost does not have flesh and bones, as you see I have" (Luke 24:39). Earlier that resurrection morning Mary of Magdala had apparently embraced the resurrected Jesus (John 20:17), and when Jesus appeared to the women and greeted them, "they came to him, clasped his feet and worshiped him" (Matt. 28:9).

Further evidence of the physical reality of Jesus' resurrection body is the fact that He ate food. Luke reported that He ate broiled fish (Luke 24:42). Although Luke did not report that Jesus ate anything with the two disciples at Emmaus, "When he was at the table with them, he took bread, gave thanks, broke it and began to give it to them" (24:30). Likewise at Jesus' appearance to the disciples along the shore of the Sea of Galilee, the

Lord had prepared "a fire of burning coal there with fish on it, and some bread" (John 21:9). Then Jesus invited them, "Come and have breakfast," and He "took the bread and gave it to them, and did the same with the fish" (21:12–13). Though John did not say Jesus ate the food, it is likely that He did.

At the same time Jesus' resurrection body had characteristics that set it apart from the normal physical body. When John appeared to the woman near the empty tomb at that resurrection morning, Matthew wrote, "Suddenly Jesus met them" (28:9), suggesting He appeared out of nowhere. That evening, "when the disciples were together, with the doors locked for fear of the Jews, Jesus came and stood among them" (John 20:19; Luke 24:36), apparently having the ability to appear at will. This also involved the ability to disappear, because, when the eyes of the Emmaus disciples "were opened, and they recognized him, he disappeared from their sight" (Luke 24:31). The incident with these two disciples also reveals the resurrected Jesus' ability to hide His identity, for "they were kept from recognizing him" (24:16), which continued until "their eyes were opened, and they recognized him" (24:31). Mary of Magdala's inability to recognize the resurrected Jesus until He called her by name (John 20:16) was probably the result more of her distraught state and tears and passing glance at the figure who spoke to her than of a supernatural hindrance to her recognition (20:14–15).

The Empty Tomb

The strongest evidence for the genuineness of Jesus' resurrection is the fact of the empty tomb. The story spread by the bribed guards that His disciples stole Jesus' body while they slept had "been widely circulated among the Jews" (Matt. 28:15). This story was obviously false. If the disciples had stolen the body, why were they willing to suffer persecution and death for their proclamation of Jesus' resurrection?

Modern skeptics have insisted that Mary of Magdala and the other women in the early morning darkness simply went to the wrong tomb and had hallucinations of seeing angels and Jesus. But when Joseph of Arimathea placed Jesus' body "in his own new tomb" (27:60), "Mary

Magdalene and the other Mary were sitting there opposite the tomb" (27:61). Mark wrote, "Mary Magdalene and Mary the mother of Joses saw where he was laid" (Mark 15:47), and Luke said, "The women who had come with Jesus from Galilee followed Joseph and saw the tomb and how the body was laid in it" (Luke 23:15). So they certainly knew where He was buried.

That they went to the wrong tomb takes a long stretch of the imagination. If we accept that idea, Simon Peter and John also went to the wrong tomb (John 20:2–4). Not only that, but the "strips of linen" (20:5–7) and the "burial cloth" (20:7) also were at the wrong tomb. When the disciples began preaching Jesus' resurrection, all the Roman guards or authorities or Jewish leaders would need to have done was go to the correct tomb, open it, and show Jesus' body, easily identifiable by the wounds of His crucifixion. In fact, Joseph, the owner of the tomb, even though a secret disciple, could have done the same thing.

The Lord's Resurrection Appearances

Luke declared that Jesus "showed himself to these men [the apostles] and gave many convincing proofs that he was alive. He appeared to them over a period of forty days" (Acts 1:3). Ryrie lists ten separate resurrection appearances of Christ,[1] actually eleven if the appearance on the day of Ascension is counted separately. Five of these were on the day of resurrection and the rest in the forty days of resurrection ministry. The apostle Paul also included Jesus' appearance to him on the road to Damascus (Acts 9:3–7), even though it occurred after our Lord's ascension (1 Cor. 15:8–9). Another postascension appearance is the one to the first martyr Stephen (Acts 7:55–56). Ryrie concludes, "In all, 538 (549 if the eleven, Matt. 28:16, be distinct from the 500 [1 Cor. 15:6]) persons are *specified* as having seen the risen savior."[2] This implies that other appearances to still more persons may have occurred, which may well be true.

Modern skeptics dismiss the biblical accounts of the resurrection appearances of Jesus as hallucinations brought on psychologically by the disciples' intense desire and hope for Jesus to be still alive. According to Scripture the psychological mood of Jesus' followers was the exact opposite. After seeing "the tomb and how his body was laid in it," the women "went home and prepared spices and perfumes" (Luke 23:55–56). Mark reported that "when the Sabbath was over, Mary Magdalene, Mary the mother of James, and Salome bought spices so that they might go to anoint Jesus' body" (Mark 16:1), asking each other, "Who will roll the stone away from the entrance of the tomb?" (16:3; see Luke 24:1). Clearly they were not anticipating a resurrection.

On the resurrection morning when Mary Magdalene went "to the tomb and saw the stone had been removed from the entrance" (John 20:1), she ran to Simon Peter and the other disciple and told them, "They have taken the Lord out of the tomb, and we don't know where they have put him!" (20:2). She did not say, "Jesus has been raised from the dead." When she returned to the tomb, she stood outside it, crying (20:11). When the angels inside the tomb asked her why she was crying, she replied, "They have taken my Lord away . . . and I don't know where they have put him" (20:13). Then when Jesus appeared to her and asked the same question, she thought He was the gardener. So "she said, 'Sir, if you have carried him away, tell me where you have put him, and I will get him'" (20:15). At no time did she assume Jesus had been resurrected until she was convinced by His appearance to her.

The same attitude of sadness and despondency is seen in the two disciples on the Emmaus road. When Jesus approached them and asked what they were discussing (Luke 24:16–17), "they stood still, their faces downcast" (24:17). Even though they had heard reports that Jesus was alive (24:22–24), they obviously were not filled with hope of His resurrection. Even after the other apostles told Thomas of seeing the resurrected Jesus, Thomas doubted (John 20:24–28). Likewise, when "the eleven disciples went to Galilee, to the mountain where Jesus had told them to go" (Matt. 28:16; 28:7, 10), Matthew continued, "When they saw him, they worshiped him; but some doubted" (28:17). Rather than experiencing psychologically induced illusions of Jesus' resurrection, the disciples had to be convinced of its reality by "many convincing proofs that he was alive" (Acts 1:3).

The *coup de grace* to the skeptics' argument that Jesus' resurrection appearances were psychologically induced hallucinations is Paul's report that "he appeared to more than five hundred of the brothers at the same time, most of whom are still living" (1 Cor. 15:6). Hallucinations such as visions of the Virgin Mary are individual experiences, occurring to one person at a time, although possibly experienced by different individuals at different times. The resurrected Jesus' appearance to more than five hundred people at once cannot be explained as a hallucination; it must be true.

GLORIFIED IN ASCENSION

When Jesus' mission on earth was completed with His sacrificial death and resurrection (John 17:4; 19:30), He was glorified by His being ascended to the place of honor at the right hand of God the Father in heaven (John 17:5). When Luke wrote of Jesus going to Jerusalem to die, for example, he described it as "the time . . . for him to be taken up to heaven" (Luke 9:51). Jesus' resurrection appearances and ministry of instruction to His disciples (Matt. 28:18–20; Luke 24:25–27; John 21:15–19; Acts 1:3–8), necessary and important as they were, were only a temporary "interruption" on His journey from the cross to the crown.

A number of factors show the significance of the resurrected Jesus Christ making a public, visible ascension from earth to heaven. First, the disciples needed to know with certainty that He had left them. He had been with them for forty days since His resurrection, apparently appearing now and then to an individual or a group but not with them constantly as He was before His death. They needed to know that they would no longer have the Lord's personal presence, but would have the Holy Spirit's power for their witness and ministry as Christ's representatives (Matt. 28:18–20; John 14:16, 26; 16:7–15; Acts 1:4–5, 7–8).

Second, the disciples needed to see Jesus ascend to heaven in His immortal, resurrection body, because this is the way Christians as members of Christ's body, the church, will ascend to heaven in the Rapture (1 Cor. 15:51–58; 1 Thess. 4:16–18).

Third, the disciples needed to watch as Jesus "was taken up before their very eyes, and a cloud hid him from their sight" (Acts 1:9; see Mark 16:19; Luke 24:51), and to hear the words of the angels, "This same Jesus, who has been taken from you into heaven, will come back in the same way you have seen him go into heaven" (Acts 1:11). This promise of the ascended Lord Jesus' return to the earth relates to His second coming to establish His kingdom of righteousness and peace on David's throne. This promise does not refer to the Rapture, His coming in the air to take His church to be with Him; at His second coming, His bodily appearance will be evident to the world ("Behold, He is coming with the clouds, and every eye will see him," Rev. 1:7, NKJV), but at the Rapture only church age saints will see Him. With His ascension to the right hand of God the Father in heaven the first coming of the incarnate Son of God ended and His present session began.

Nine

CHRIST'S PRESENT MINISTRY AT
THE RIGHT HAND OF GOD THE FATHER

As a boy of twelve, having trusted the Lord Jesus Christ as my Savior, I faced the problem of repeatedly yielding to temptation and falling into sin. I would be filled with guilt and remorse and would vow not to sin again, but invariably I would. It was frustrating and I wondered why the Lord did not help me resist. In my daily Bible reading I had learned that the glorified Jesus had been "exalted to the right hand of God" (Acts 2:33; 5:31; Eph. 1:20; Col. 3:1), where "he sat down at the right hand of God" (Heb. 10:12; 8:1; 12:2). In my childish mind I pictured Him sitting there at ease, twiddling His thumbs and doing nothing to help me in my dilemma. Fortunately, as my knowledge of the Bible expanded and I grew as a Christian, I learned of the Lord's provision of the Holy Spirit and of Christ's present ministry for His own at the right hand of God the Father. Yielding to the Holy Spirit's control and availing myself of the present ministry of my Lord have not made me free of sin, but they have helped me to live a victorious Christian life.

CHRIST'S POSITION AT GOD'S RIGHT HAND

In the ancient world the seat at the right hand of a monarch was the place of honor. It was given to a victorious general or to a wise and faithful counselor. It has been rightfully awarded to the Lord Jesus as the One who has completed the task God gave Him (John 17:4)—the One who by His death on Calvary's cross defeated Satan, sin, and death. David had written, "The LORD says to my Lord, 'Sit at my right hand until I make your enemies a footstool for your feet'" (Ps. 110:1). Jesus Himself referred to this passage when He debated with the Pharisees concerning His identity as the Christ. To His question, "Whose son is he?" they correctly responded, "The son of David" (Matt. 22:42; Mark 12:35). Seeking to show them that He was more than a human being, Jesus asked, "How is it then that David, speaking by the Spirit, calls him 'Lord'?" (Matt. 22:43). Then He quoted Psalm 110:1 and asked, "If then David calls him 'Lord,' how can he be his son?" (Matt. 22:44–45; Mark 12:36–37). Similarly, in his sermon on the Day of Pentecost, the apostle Peter pointed out that "David did not ascend to heaven," and then Peter quoted Psalm 110:1 as a prophecy of the exaltation of Jesus (Acts 2:34).

Of importance is the fact that the throne at God's right hand is the throne of God the Father, not Jesus' throne. The author of the epistle to the Hebrews wrote that Jesus "sat down at the right hand of the throne of God" (12:2; see 8:1; Matt. 5:34; 23:22; Acts 7:49). The glorified Christ in His messages to the seven churches through the apostle John said, "To him who overcomes, I will give the right to sit with me on my throne, just as I overcame and sat down with my Father on his throne" (Rev. 3:21). Furthermore, the exalted Jesus is to remain at God the Father's right hand as the honored One until God fulfills His promise to "make His enemies a footstool for His feet" (Pss. 110:1; see Matt. 22:44; Mark 12:36). Our Lord's present activity in building and ministering to His church is separate from and does not compromise His remaining at God's right hand until that promise is fulfilled.

The promoters of a position called progressive dispensationalism view Jesus' position at God's right hand differently. Its exponents are dispensationalists because "they view the church as a *new manifestation of grace,* a new dispensation in the history of redemption,"[1] and they affirm that "the church is a new institution, begun at Pentecost."[2] At the same time, however, they insist that "Jesus' rule from God's right hand initially yet decisively fulfills promises made to David."[3] They recognize a future millennial dispensation with Christ reigning visibly on earth in Jerusalem on David's throne with Israel as the head of the nations; but now, "As the Davidic heir, Jesus sits in and rules from heaven."[4] As a result they believe that both the dispensation of Christ's present ministry from heaven and the future millennial dispensation are "united as aspects of the messianic reign of Christ."[5] "*Both* dispensations are seen in the New Testament as fulfillments of the Davidic covenant."[6]

The difference of opinion begins in progressive dispensationalism's teaching concerning Jesus' presentation of Himself as the promised Messiah in His ministry on earth in the first Advent. According to this view, Jesus' presentation of Himself to the Jewish people inaugurated His messianic kingdom. "In the gospel of Luke, it is clear that with Jesus' presence, and especially in his Resurrection-Ascension, comes the beginning of Jesus' kingdom." And "first, there is an inauguration with Jesus' coming and particularly in his resurrection-ascension to [sic] God's right hand."[7]

In support of the position that Christ's presence marked the inauguration of His messianic kingdom, progressive dispensationalists point to Jesus' miracles of healing the sick, giving sight to the blind, enabling the lame to walk, and raising the dead. Jesus told John the Baptist's disciples to describe these miracles to John as confirming evidence that He was "the one who was to come" (Matt. 11:3), the Christ, the One whom John had announced (3:2, 11–12). No one questions the fact that such miracles demonstrate Jesus' identity as Israel's Messiah, but performing miracles is not the same as marking the inauguration of His messianic kingdom. Instead the miracles identified Him as the Messiah in His offer of Himself as such to the Jewish people.

As His ministry continued, the Jewish religious leaders increasingly opposed Jesus and rejected Him as their Messiah until Caiaphas, "high priest that year" (John 11:49), told the Sanhedrin, "it is better for you that one man die for the people than that the whole nation perish" (11:50). John continued, "So from that day on they plotted to take his life" (11:53). Speaking of the Jewish people at Jerusalem in particular, John later wrote, "Even after Jesus had done all these miraculous signs in their presence, they still would not believe in him" (12:37). This rejection, John noted, fulfilled Isaiah 53:1, which he quoted. The Jewish people's rejection of

Jesus as their Messiah was final when Pilate presented Jesus to the crowd as their King and the crowd shouted, "Take him away! Crucify him!" and the chief priests said, "We have no king but Caesar" (John 19:15). In the face of such rejection of the King by His subjects, the kingdom can hardly have been inaugurated.

Progressive dispensationalism makes much of Peter's statement that the miracle of the disciples speaking in tongues as a result of the filling of the Holy Spirit on the Day of Pentecost was "what was spoken by the prophet Joel" (Acts 2:16). They quote Joel 2:28–32, pointing out that the beginning of the present dispensation of the church is identified as part of "the last days" (Acts 2:17). This is not quite correct, however, because "the last days" are Peter's words, not Joel's, who said, "And afterward" (Joel 2:28). Progressive dispensationalists are partially correct, however, because the writer to the Hebrews used the phrase "in these last days" in relationship to Jesus' incarnation and first coming (Heb. 1:2). Although the outpouring of the Holy Spirit at Pentecost *corresponds* to what Joel prophesied, he was speaking about an outpouring in the dark days immediately preceding the second coming of Christ to earth (Joel 2:30–31), not the outpouring to begin the church.

Progressive dispensationalism also focuses on Peter's quotation at Pentecost from two of David's psalms (Pss. 16:8–11; 110:1) that speak prophetically of Jesus' resurrection in a body that did not experience decay. They draw the conclusion that since by resurrection and ascension "God has made this Jesus, whom you crucified, both Lord and Christ" (Acts 2:36), He is now fulfilling the Davidic Covenant and reigning in heaven. True, Jesus is David's greater Son (Luke 1:32), but the focus of the Davidic Covenant is God's promise to David that "your house [i.e., lineage] and your kingdom will endure forever before me; your throne will be established forever" (2 Sam. 7:16; see 7:13; Ps. 89:28–29, 34–37) on earth, and not in heaven. Christ is not now fulfilling the Davidic Covenant; instead He is now at God's right hand, waiting "for his enemies to be made his footstool" (Heb. 10:13; see Ps. 110:1). In the future He will return to earth to occupy David's throne and fulfill God's promises to David.

In a real sense what Peter did both in his message on the Day of Pentecost and more specifically in his sermon in Solomon's Colonnade (Acts

3:11–26) was to call the Jewish people to repent and to accept Jesus as their Messiah so that He could return and establish His messianic kingdom. In effect it was a reoffer of the kingdom. Peter said, "Repent, then, and turn to God, so that your sins may be wiped out, that times of refreshing may come from the Lord, and *that he may send the Christ, who has been appointed for you—even Jesus.* He must remain in heaven until the time comes for God to restore everything, as he promised long ago through his holy prophets" (3:19–21, italics added). Though many individual Jews responded to Peter's message ("about three thousand" on the Day of Pentecost; 2:41) and the apostles' witness ("the Lord added to their number daily those who were being saved"; 2:47), the Jewish religious leaders rejected His message and increasingly persecuted the apostles (4:3, 5–7, 18–21; 5:17–27, 41) and others, resulting in the martyrdom of Stephen (6:12; 7:54–60) and greatly increased persecution that dispersed all of the believers except the apostles (8:1, 3).

Progressive dispensationalists, together with the adherents of what they call "revised dispensationalism,"[8] accept a single New Covenant instituted by Christ with the Twelve at the Passover Feast the evening before His arrest and death (Matt. 26:17–20, 26–29; Mark 14:12–17, 22–25; Luke 22:7–20), and commemorated by His church in the Lord's Supper (1 Cor. 11:23–26) as a proclamation of "the Lord's death until he comes" (11:26). For the people of Israel, represented by the Twelve, the New Covenant will become effective with the establishment of the messianic kingdom at Christ's return to earth. Jesus told the Twelve, "I will not drink of this fruit of the vine from now on until the day when I drink it anew with you in my Father's kingdom" (Matt. 26:29; Mark 14:25; Luke 22:16, 18). At that future time the blessings of the New Covenant will be bestowed on the repentant, redeemed people of Israel as prophesied by Moses (Deut. 30:1–10) and the prophets (Isa. 11:10–12:6; 14:1–3; 25:6–9; 26:1–27:13; 59:20–60:22; Jer. 31:1–25, 37:1–23; Dan. 2:44–45; 7:15–18, 23–27; 12:1–2; Joel 2–3). Although some blessings of the New Covenant now enjoyed by members of Christ's body, His church, are the same as some to be bestowed on redeemed Israel in the messianic kingdom, Israel will also experience many different blessings then.

Also progressive dispensationalism identifies the spiritual blessings of the New Covenant with God's promises to David in the Davidic Covenant. However, nothing of a spiritual nature is mentioned in the promises of the Davidic Covenant; the promises deal only with a house (lineage), a kingdom, and a throne being established and enduring forever (2 Sam. 7:16; Ps. 89:28–29, 33–37). True, the spiritual blessings of the New Covenant will be poured out on the people of Israel in conjunction with the establishment of the messianic kingdom. But this is not because those blessings are part of the promises of the Davidic Covenant; rather, they will occur because of Israel's repentance and return in faith to the Lord.

Progressive dispensationalism makes the same mistake in tying the spiritual blessings of the New Covenant to the promises of the Abrahamic Covenant (Gen. 17:1–8; 15:18–20). God did tell Abram, "you will be a blessing . . . and all peoples on earth will be blessed through you" (12:2–3). Abraham also is a blessing as the stellar Old Testament example of justification by faith (15:4–6; Rom. 4:1–25; Gal. 3:6–9). God's specific promises to him in the covenant, however, were that his offspring would be as the stars of the heavens (Gen. 15:5) and that God would give "the whole land of Canaan . . . as an everlasting possession to you and your descendants after you" (17:8; see 15:18). When Israel returns to the land of Canaan and occupies it as an everlasting possession in the millennial kingdom age, they will experience the spiritual blessings of the New Covenant, blessings which are an outgrowth of the promises in the Abrahamic Covenant and, in particular the promise that "all peoples on earth will be blessed through you" (12:3).

In Hebrews 7:4–10:25 the New Covenant is contrasted with the Mosaic Covenant and the system of sacrifices, offerings, and Levitical priesthood related to that covenant. It is new as the replacement of the old Mosaic Covenant (8:8–13; Jer. 31:31–34). The New Covenant also is identified with a better high priest, one "in the order of Melchizedek" (Heb. 6:20). This new high priest is the Lord Jesus, of course, who "did not take upon himself the glory of becoming a high priest" (5:5) but "was designated by God to be high priest in the order of Melchizedek" (5:10). God the Father said to Him, "You are a priest forever, in the order of Melchizedek" (5:6; see 7:21; Ps. 110:4).

Since "Melchizedek was king of Salem and priest of God Most High" (Heb. 7:1; Gen. 14:18) and Christ is a priest "in the order of Melchizedek," progresssive dispensationalists tie Christ's priestly work of bestowing blessings together with His being the Davidic king and conclude that He is now bestowing those blessings as part of His reign as the Davidic king in heaven. They believe that "the Melchizedekian priesthood is part of the Davidic Covenant"[9] simply on the basis of the inclusion of the statement, "You are a priest forever, in the order of Melchizedek" (Ps. 110:4) in the same psalm as the statement, "The LORD says to my Lord; 'Sit at my right hand until I make your enemies a footstool for your feet'" (110:1). However, no reference to the Davidic Covenant is made in the psalm, nor is either statement a promise in the Davidic Covenant. They also believe that "the Melchizedekian priesthood is an office given to David's son as part of his inheritance."[10] But nowhere does the Bible state that the Melchizedekian priesthood is part of the inheritance of Christ, David's Descendant.

In addition, Melchizedek ministered to Abram as "priest of God Most High" approximately a thousand years before David's reign. Therefore instead of the Melchizedekian priesthood being an office given to David's Son as part of His inheritance, as progressive dispensationalism states, the reverse is true: Being David's Son is an honor given to Christ, the Melchizedekian Priest, as part of His inheritance. Progressive dispensationalism, however, says that Christ's bestowal of spiritual blessings now are part of His reign as the Davidic King in heaven. Further, although Melchizedek was "king of Salem," he ministered to Abram, blessed him and God Most High, and received "a tenth of everything" from Abram as priest of God Most High (Gen. 14:18–20). Since Abram was not a resident of Salem, Melchizedek had no real relationship to him. Also being a king does not necessarily mean functioning as a king. Christ is King now, but He is not now reigning as the Davidic King, fulfilling the Davidic Covenant. David was anointed as king of Israel by Samuel (1 Sam. 16:1, 12–13) more than fifteen years before he was publicly anointed as king over Judah and seven and a-half more years before he was publicly anointed as king of all Israel (2 Sam. 5:2–5; 1 Chron. 11:1–3; 12:38). Certainly, therefore, Jesus Christ as David's Son and Heir can now be the Davidic King without functioning as such until He returns to earth and establishes the kingdom.

In many respects the crux of the difference of opinion with progressive dispensationalism focuses on its interpretation of the statements in Psalm 110:1, 4, the quotation of Psalm 110:1 by Peter in Acts 2:34–35, and the relationship of those verses to the fulfillment of the Davidic Covenant. In an excellent article on the interpretation of Psalm 110, Elliott Johnson writes, "Is Jesus' present position at God's right hand one of royal, Davidic status? Several observations about Psalm 110:1 and Peter's quotation of it in Acts 2:34–35 help show that the answer to that question is no: *1. The Messiah's present seating awaits a future conquest. . . . 2. The Messiah's present position does not include the images of coronation. . . . 3. The Messiah's present seating involves what Yahweh decreed.*"[11] In contradiction to progressive dispensationalism Johnson concludes from Psalm 110 that "Messiah's present session does not involve His reigning on David's throne."[12]

CHRIST'S PRESENT MINISTRY
THROUGH THE HOLY SPIRIT

Jesus had been announced by John the Baptist as the One who "will baptize you with the Holy Spirit and with fire" (Matt. 3:11; Mark 1:8; Luke 3:16). Jesus Himself instructed the apostles about the coming ministry of the Holy Spirit. The evening before His arrest and crucifixion He explained to them, "It is for your good that I am going away. Unless I go away, the Counselor [the Holy Spirit, John 14:16–17] will not come to you; but if I go, I will send him to you" (John 16:7). Later John recorded that in His appearance to the apostles the evening of His resurrection Jesus commissioned them, saying, "'As the Father has sent me, I am sending you.' And with that he breathed on them and said, 'Receive the Holy Spirit'" (20:21–22). This gift of the Holy Spirit before the Day of Pentecost apparently was to enable the apostles to understand Jesus' life, ministry, death, and resurrection and to relate these events to the Old Testament prophecies of them in preparation for Pentecost and what followed (see Luke 24:8; John 12:16; 2:17, 22).

During His postresurrection ministry Jesus instructed His disciples, "Do not leave Jerusalem, but wait for the gift my Father promised, which you have heard me speak about. For John baptized with water, but in a few days you will be baptized with the Holy Spirit" (Acts 1:4–5). Just before His ascension Jesus told the disciples in response to their question about restoring "the kingdom to Israel" (1:6), "But you will receive power when the Holy Spirit comes on you; and you will be my witnesses in Jerusalem, and in all Judea and Samaria, and to the ends of the earth" (1:8). This baptism with the Holy Spirit occurred on the Day of Pentecost and is described by Peter as "what was spoken by the prophet Joel" (2:16–21; see Joel 2:28–32).

The Beginning of Christ's Church

Although the outpouring of the Holy Spirit on the Day of Pentecost corresponds to part of Joel's prophecy, it also marks something totally unique in God's eternal plan, the beginning of the church of the Lord Jesus Christ made up of those who are joined with Him as members of His body by the baptism of the Holy Spirit (1 Cor. 12:13; Gal. 3:27–28; Eph. 4:4–5). The beginning of the church on Pentecost is symbolically significant, because that day in Israel marked the offering of firstfruits (Lev. 23:15–21). Although the baptism by the Holy Spirit into the body of Christ at the moment of saving faith is itself nonexperimental in the sense that it is not accompanied by any outward signs, on the Day of Pentecost it was accompanied by a "sound like the blowing of a violent wind came from heaven," "tongues of fire that separated and came to rest on each of them," the filling "with the Holy Spirit," and speaking "in other tongues as the Spirit enabled them" (Acts 2:1–4). These spectacular signs marked the beginning of the church and served as a witness to the Jewish people, as Peter explained in his sermon.

Jesus Himself had foretold the beginning of His church as a new thing when He responded to Peter's confession of Him as "the Christ, the Son of the living God" (Matt. 16:16) with the declaration, "on this rock I will build my church" (16:18). The use of the future tense "will build" indicates that Christ's church is something new, not just a continuation or variation of the nation of Israel as God's chosen people. This is why the church made up of Jews and Gentiles with equal standing as members of the body of

Christ (1 Cor. 12:13; Gal. 3:27–28) was described by the apostle Paul as a mystery (Eph. 3:3–12; 5:32; Col. 1:25–27)—something hidden and not known in the past but now clearly and fully revealed and proclaimed.

Although the church began on Pentecost, its true character came to be understood by its leaders only gradually, because at first it was composed only of Jews. Peter was introduced to the true nature of the church by his visit to Cornelius, a Gentile convert to Judaism (Acts 10:1–2), and his vision and instruction from God not to "call anything impure that God has made clean" (10:15). When "the Holy Spirit came on all who heard the message . . . while Peter was still speaking" (10:44), he "ordered that they be baptized in the name of Jesus Christ" (10:48), because, Peter said, "they have received the Holy Spirit just as we have" (10:47). Here again the baptism of the Holy Spirit was accompanied by "speaking in tongues and praising God" as outward evidence to Peter and his companions of its occurrence. When Peter was criticized when he returned to Jerusalem, he explained everything that had happened and said, "So if God gave them the same gift as he gave us, who believed in the Lord Jesus Christ, who was I to think that I could oppose God?" (11:17). The assembly agreed, saying, "So then, God has even granted the Gentiles repentance unto life" (11:18).

The next and final step in recognizing the unique character of Christ's church came when Paul and Barnabas returned to Antioch in Syria from their first missionary journey "and reported all that God had done through them and how he had opened the door of faith to the Gentiles" (14:27). This raised the issue of how the Gentile believers were to be received, because Cornelius, although a Gentile, had already become a proselyte to Judaism before receiving Christ. Some visitors to Antioch from Judea insisted, "Unless you are circumcised according to the custom taught by Moses, you cannot be saved" (15:1). But Paul and Barnabas disputed this position (15:2), because it meant that believers had to become identified with Judaism in order to be Christians. This would have made the church a branch of Judaism.

The issue was taken to Jerusalem, where "the apostles and elders met to consider this question" (15:6) of whether "the Gentiles must be circumcised and required to obey the law of Moses" (15:5). Peter reminded them of his experience with Cornelius and concluded, "Now then, why do you try to test God by putting on the necks of the disciples a yoke that neither we nor our fathers have been able to bear? No! We believe it is through the grace of our Lord Jesus that we are saved, just as they are" (15:10–11). Then, after Barnabas and Paul recounted their experiences, James indicated that Peter's experience was supported by the Old Testament prophets, in effect quoting Amos 9:11–12. James recommended that they "not make it difficult for the Gentiles who are turning to God" but should write them, "telling them to abstain from food polluted by idols, from sexual immorality, from meat of strangled animals and from blood" (15:19–20). In this way they would avoid offending Jews scattered throughout the Roman Empire (15:21).

This emphasis of Scripture on the uniqueness of the church, the body of Christ, as a mystery of God hidden from past ages—in the Old Testament—is why it is wrong for progressive dispensationalism to identify the ministry of the Holy Spirit and the present session of Christ with His reigning at God's right hand as the Davidic King in initial fulfillment of the Davidic Covenant. This blurs the uniqueness of the church, even though progressive dispensationalism insists that the church is a new institution begun at Pentecost.

Sending the Counselor

During His public ministry the Lord Jesus was almost the constant companion of His disciples, from His calling them to follow Him (John 1:43; Matt. 4:19–22; 9:9) to His ascension to God's right hand. This was in the pattern of the Jewish rabbi, "which means Teacher" (John 1:38), a title used of Jesus (1:49; 3:2; 4:31; 6:25; Matt. 23:7–10; see John 20:16) and of John the Baptist (John 3:26). As they traveled and preached the gospel of the kingdom of heaven, Jesus taught both the public and His disciples (Matt. 5:1–2; 7:28–29; 24:3; Luke 24:25–27; Acts 1:3).

While on earth, however, Jesus was limited by His physical body. To send His disciples to be His "witnesses . . . to the ends of the earth" (Acts 1:8; see Matt. 28:19; Luke 24:47–48) required His glorification to God's right hand and His empowerment of the disciples through the Holy Spirit. As Jesus told them, "I tell you the truth: It is for your good that I am going away. Unless I go away, the Counselor will not come to you; but if I go, I will send him to you" (John 16:7). Just before He ascended to heaven Jesus told them, "You will receive power when the Holy Spirit comes on you" (Acts 1:8).

In John's Gospel Jesus taught the apostles about His sending the Holy Spirit and the Spirit's ministry to them. The Greek noun for Counselor is *parakletos,* frequently simply transliterated Paraclete. It literally means "called to one's aid" (in a judicial sense) and therefore it is frequently translated "an advocate, pleader, intercessor,"[13] in which sense it is used of the Lord Jesus (1 John 2:1) with God the Father. Jesus called the Holy Spirit "another Counselor," whom He said the Father would give the disciples in response to His request to be with them forever (John 14:16). The word "another" is significant, because it means another of the same kind, in other words, one like Christ.

Jesus explained that the Holy Spirit would be not only the disciples' Companion and Intercessor but also their Teacher, reminding them of everything Jesus had said to them (14:26). Later Jesus told them, "When the Counselor comes, whom I will send to you from the Father, the Spirit of Truth who goes out from the Father, he will testify about me" (15:26). Still later He said, "I have much more to say to you, more than you can now bear. But when he, the Spirit of truth, comes, he will guide you into all truth. He will not speak on his own; he will speak only what he hears, and he will tell you what is yet to come. He will bring glory to me by taking from what is mine and making it known to you. All that belongs to the Father is mine. That is why I said the Spirit will take from what is mine and make it known to you" (16:12–15).

The Lord Jesus said He would send the Holy Spirit not only to minister both to and through His followers but also to minister to the unsaved. He told the apostles, "When he comes, he will convict the world of guilt in regard to sin and righteousness and judgment: in regard to sin, because men do not believe in me; in regard to righteousness, because I am going to the Father, where you can see me no longer; and in regard to judgment, because the prince of this world now stands condemned" (16:8–11). As Blum explains, "Conviction is not the same as conversion but is necessary to it. . . . The Spirit works on the minds of the unsaved to show them the truth of God for what it is. Normally this process includes human aid (see 15:26–27)."[14]

CHRIST'S MINISTRY AS HEAD OF HIS BODY, THE CHURCH

The spiritual relationship established between Jesus Christ and everyone who believes in Him—His church—through the ministry of the Holy Spirit is described biblically in several ways. One of the most graphic is that of a body, with Christ as its Head, because it portrays not only the relationship between Christ, the Head, and the members of the body but also among the members. Drawing the parallel to a physical body, Paul explained, "The body is a unit, though it is made up of many parts, and though all its parts are many, they form one body. So it is with Christ. For we were all baptized by one Spirit into one body—whether Jews or Greeks, slave or free—and we were all given the one Spirit to drink" (1 Cor. 12:12–13). As a result of the Holy Spirit's presence and ministry in believers as members of Christ's body, "There are different kinds of gifts, but the same Spirit. . . . Now to each one the manifestation of the Spirit is given for the common good. . . . All these are the work of one and the same Spirit, and he gives them to each man, just as he determines" (12:4, 7, 11).

Paul graphically described the interrelationship and interdependence of the parts of the body on each other. On the one hand, if all the members were only one part, how would it exercise the other functions of the body (12:14–20)? On the other hand, no part of the body can say to another part, "I don't need you!" because all are indispensable, especially the weaker (12:21–26). Paul concluded this illustration with the application, "Now you are the body of Christ, and each one of you is a part of it" (12:27). Elsewhere Paul wrote, "Just as each of us has one body with many members, and these members do not all have the same function, so in Christ we who are many form one body, and each member belongs to all the others" (Rom. 12:4–5), and "there is one body and one Spirit" (Eph. 4:4).

Lest undue emphasis be placed on the Holy Spirit and His ministry, however, we must always remember that He ministers as the Representative of and in the place of the glorified Christ at God's right hand. As Christ said concerning the Spirit before He left the apostles, He "will testify about me" (John 15:26) and "He will bring glory to me" (16:14). The glorified Christ is always "the head of the body, the church" (Col. 1:18, 24; Eph. 4:15), and as a result He directs the growth of His body (Eph. 4:16; Col. 2:19) and distributes gifts to its members (Rom. 12:6–8; 1 Cor. 12:12–31; Eph. 4:7–8, 11–13; Col. 3:15). Our Lord distributes the gifts through the Holy Spirit (1 Cor. 12:4–11), but He Himself is the directing Head (Eph. 4:4–7).

The glorified Christ is concerned, as a result, about what happens to the members of the church, His body. When the members of the Sanhedrin were stung by Stephen's bold accusations and "were furious and gnashed their teeth as him" (Acts 7:54), he "looked up to heaven and saw the glory of God, and Jesus standing at the right hand of God" (7:55). When he described what he saw, "they covered their ears and, yelling at the top of their voices, they all rushed at him, dragged him out of the city and began to stone him" (7:57–58). Later, when Saul of Tarsus was on his way to Damascus "breathing out murderous threats against the Lord's disciples" (9:1), the glorified Christ stopped him on the road with "a light from heaven" (9:3) and asked, "Saul, Saul, why do you persecute me?" (9:4). To Saul's question, "Who are you, Lord?" Christ responded, "I am Jesus, whom you are persecuting" (9:5). Persecution and harm to a Christian is persecution and harm to our glorified Lord.

CHRIST'S MINISTRY AS THE GREAT HIGH PRIEST

As the promised Great High Priest "in the order of Melchizedek" (Ps. 110:4; Heb. 5:6, 10; 6:20; 7:11, 17, 21), the glorified Christ now carries out this priestly ministry at the right hand of God. Although Scripture indicates that Christ "became the source of eternal salvation for all who obey him and was designated by God to be the high priest in the order of Melchizedek" (5:9–10) and that "he has become a high priest forever, in the order of Melchizedek" (6:20), it also says that "when this priest had offered for all time one sacrifice for sins, he sat down at the right hand of God" (10:12; see 7:27; 9:26). This implies that He was ministering as a priest in His crucifixion.

If Jesus was not ministering as a priest during His earthly ministry, He was preparing for it, because the writer of Hebrews stated, "He had to be made like his brothers in every way, in order that he might become a merciful and faithful high priest in service to God, and that he might make atonement for the sins of the people. Because he himself suffered when he was tempted, he is able to help those who are being tempted" (Heb. 2:17–18). Later the writer added, "Therefore, since we have a great high priest who has gone through the heavens, Jesus the Son of God, let us hold firmly to the faith we profess. For we do not have a high priest who is unable to sympathize with our weaknesses, but we have one who has been tempted in every way, just as we are—yet was without sin" (4:14–15). Perhaps, like the Aaronic priests, Jesus was a priest from conception and birth, or at least from His anointing with the Holy Spirit and the beginning of His public ministry at His baptism by John.

The Intercessor

The supreme work of Christ as the Great High Priest, of course, is "to do away with sin by the sacrifice of himself" (Heb. 9:26; see 7:27). Another important present ministry, however, is His receiving believers' prayers and supplications for "mercy and find grace to help us in our time of need" (4:16). Furthermore, "he is able to save completely those who come to God through him, because he always lives to intercede for them" (7:25; see 9:24; Rom. 8:34). The classic illustration of that intercession is Jesus' prayer to God the Father, recorded in John 17.

The accessibility of our Lord Jesus as the Christian's Intercessor and the constancy of His intercession for believers with God the Father make the use of the Virgin Mary as well as a galaxy of saints not only unnecessary but actually an affront to the Lord and His ministry. Jesus Christ is the "one mediator between God and men" (1 Tim. 2:5), and He and the Holy Spirit (Rom. 8:26–27) are the only intercessors. Christians have the privilege as well as the responsibility to pray for others as well as themselves, but all our prayers are to be directed to God the Father in the name of the Lord Jesus (John 16:23–24).

The Advocate

In addition to being the Christians' heavenly Intercessor, the Lord Jesus is also our Advocate with God the Father. The apostle John wrote, "My dear children, I write this to you so that you will not sin. But if anybody does sin, we have one who speaks to the Father in our defense—Jesus Christ the Righteous One" (1 John 2:1). The phrase "one who speaks in our defense" translates the same Greek noun, *paraklētos,* that was described earlier as applied to the Holy Spirit.

The first time I heard Lewis Sperry Chafer speak, his message was on this passage and its context. He pointed out that Christ was not the typical defense attorney, because, in exercising His office, He has the title "the Righteous One." Jesus has the perfect defense: "He is the atoning sacrifice for our sins, and not only for ours but also for the sins of the whole world" (2:2). As an entering student at Dallas Seminary, I was impressed by this truth, because this issue of my sin and how to deal with it had disturbed me as a youth and an immature Christian. From the context Chafer pointed out how to deal with sin. To "claim to be without sin" is to "deceive ourselves" (1:8). To "claim we have not sinned" is "to make him out to be a liar" (1:10). But, "If we confess our sins, he is faithful and just and will forgive us our sins and purify us from all unrighteousness" (1:9).

CHRIST'S OTHER PRESENT MINISTRIES
AND RELATIONSHIPS

During His earthly ministry the Lord Jesus described Himself as a Shepherd, and the same imagery is used of Him in His present ministry. Jesus told a gathering of Pharisees, "I am the good shepherd. The good shepherd lays down his life for the sheep" (John 10:11). In the same discussion He told them, "I know my sheep and my sheep know me" (10:14). A bit later He said, "My sheep listen to my voice; I know them, and they follow me. I give them eternal life, and they shall never perish; no one can snatch them out of my hand" (10:27–28). To the Christian these are comforting and encouraging words. In the same general discussion Jesus called Himself "the gate for the sheep," adding that "whoever enters through me will be saved. He will come in and go out, and find pasture" (10:7, 9).

In Hebrews Jesus is called "that great Shepherd of the sheep" (Heb. 13:20). Peter described his readers as having been "like sheep going astray, but now you have returned to the Shepherd and Overseer of your souls" (1 Pet. 2:25). Likewise he urged the elders in the group to "be shepherds of God's flock" (5:2–3). If they carry out these duties, "when the Chief Shepherd appears, [they] will receive the crown of glory that will never fade away" (5:4).

In the Gospels Jesus also referred to Himself by quoting the Old Testament to the effect that "the stone the builders rejected has become the capstone; the Lord has done this, and it is marvelous in our eyes" (Matt. 21:42; Mark 12:10–11; Ps. 118:22–23; see Luke 20:17). Paul developed this relationship between Christ and His church when he wrote that we are "built on the foundation of the apostles and prophets, with Christ Jesus himself as the chief cornerstone. In him the whole building is joined together and rises to become a holy temple in the Lord. And in him you too are being built together to become a dwelling in which God lives by his Spirit" (Eph. 2:20–22). Peter used much the same figure when he wrote, "As you come to him, the living Stone—rejected by men but chosen by God and precious to him—you also, like living stones, are being built into a spiritual house to be a holy priesthood" (1 Pet. 2:4–5).

Another relationship between Christ and His church is that of the bride and her bridegroom, as well as a husband and his wife. When John the Baptist's disciples complained to him about Jesus that "everyone is going to him" (John 3:26), John explained, "The bride belongs to the bridegroom. The friend who attends the bridegroom waits and listens for him, and is full of joy when he hears the bridegroom's voice. That joy is mine, and it is now complete" (3:29). Paul said the relationship between the husband and wife is to be like that of the relationship between Christ and the church, a relationship of love and submission (Eph. 5:22–33). When Christ returns to earth in His second coming, He will be like a bridegroom who, having taken his bride (the church) to himself, will then celebrate with a wedding banquet. "For the wedding [feast] of the Lamb has come, and his bride has made herself ready" (Rev. 19:7). An angel told John to write, "Blessed are those who are invited to the wedding supper of the Lamb" (19:9).

One other relationship between Christ and His church that is connected with His present ministry at God's right hand is that of the vine and the branches. Jesus told the apostles, "I am the vine, you are the branches. If a man remains in me and I in him, he will bear much fruit; apart from me you can do nothing. . . . This is to my Father's glory, that you bear much fruit, showing yourselves to be my disciples" (John 15:5, 8). Earlier He had explained, "I am the true vine and my Father is the gardener" (15:1), and "every branch that does bear fruit he prunes so that it will be even more fruitful" (15:2). He told them, "Remain in me, and I will remain in you. No branch can bear fruit by itself; it must remain in the vine. Neither can you bear fruit unless you remain in me " (15:4). As believers abide in fellowship with Christ, they, like branches on a grapevine, can bear fruit, that is, they can produce the qualities of godly character.

Ten

CHRIST'S TRANSLATION
OF HIS CHURCH TO HEAVEN

———◦◦◦———

ESUS' ANNOUNCEMENT to His apostles that He would be leaving them (John 13:33, 36) greatly disturbed them. To calm their agitation He told them, "Do not let your hearts be troubled. . . . In my Father's house are many rooms; if it were not so, I would have told you. I am going there to prepare a place for you. And if I go and prepare a place for you, I will come back and take you to be with me that you also may be where I am" (14:1–3). This is not a promise to take believers to heaven at the moment of death, as many teach. As Merrill Tenney wrote, "'I will come back' is one of the few allusions in this gospel to Jesus' return. . . . His return is as certain as His departure, and he would take them with him to his Father's house."[1] A. T. Robertson explains that the Greek verb translated "I will come back" is a "futuristic present middle, [a] definite promise of the Second Coming of Christ."[2]

It is important, however, to distinguish this coming of Christ to take His church to be with Him in heaven from His return to the earth to establish His kingdom. The coming that Jesus referred to in John 14:3 is the Rapture, in which the glorified Christ will "take you to be with me that you may also be where I am," that is, to heaven. In His present ministry, He is preparing places in heaven for His own.

THE RAPTURE: THE RESURRECTION
AND TRANSFORMATION OF ALL CHRISTIANS

The event known as the Rapture of the church includes the physical resurrection of all dead Christians in immortal, spiritual bodies (1 Cor. 15:35–38, 42–50) together with the transformation of all living Christians (15:51–58), and Christ's transporting them to heaven. The word *Rapture* transliterates a Latin word that means "to seize, snatch." As a result, in older English the word meant "to be carried away in body or spirit," whereas in modern-day English the word is often used to speak of an ecstatic experience. But in the Rapture the church will be physically transported to join the glorified Christ in heaven.

Believers in Thessalonica had become concerned about fellow Christians who had died. The apostle Paul wrote to them, "Brothers, we do not want you to be ignorant about those who fall asleep, or grieve like the rest of men, who have no hope" (1 Thess. 4:13). He explained, "We believe that Jesus died and rose again and so we believe that God will bring with Jesus those who have fallen asleep in him" (4:14). He continued, "According to the Lord's own word, we tell you that we who are still alive, who are left till the coming of the Lord, will certainly not precede those who have fallen asleep" (4:15). He elaborated, "For the Lord himself will come down from heaven, with a loud command, with the voice of the archangel and with the trumpet call of God, and the dead in Christ will rise first" (4:16). Someone has jokingly noted that dead Christians will be resurrected before living believers are taken up, because the former will have to travel six more feet from their graves. "After that," Paul continued, "we who are still alive and are left will be caught up with them in the clouds to meet the Lord in the air. And so we will be with the Lord forever" (4:17). His final word was, "Therefore encourage each other with these words" (4:18). These are encouraging words and good reason why Paul called the coming of Christ for the translation of His church "the blessed hope—the glorious appearing of our great God and Savior, Jesus Christ" (Titus 2:13).

This coming of Christ in the air will be limited to His church, believers of the present church age. Some Bible teachers, however, include Old Testament saints among those who will be resurrected in the Rapture.

One reason they suggest this is Paul's reference to "the voice of the arch-angel and the trumpet call of God" (1 Thess. 4:16), both of which they identify with the people of Israel, especially the archangel, Michael (Dan. 10:13, 21; 12:1; Jude 9; Rev. 12:7). In 1 Corinthians, on the other hand, Paul stated, "We will not all sleep, but we will all be changed—in a flash, in the twinkling of an eye, at the last trumpet. For the trumpet will sound, the dead will be raised imperishable, and we will be changed" (15:51–52). Here the dead are obviously the ones whom he called "the dead in Christ" in 1 Thessalonians 4:16. Furthermore, Paul introduced the truth in 1 Corinthians as "a mystery" (1 Cor. 15:51), something hidden from past ages that is now revealed. It is not likely, therefore, that it would include the resurrection of Jewish Old Testament saints. When Christ returns to earth in His second coming to establish His millennial kingdom, another phase of the "first resurrection" will occur. This will most likely be the time when Old Testament saints will be resurrected (Rev. 20:4–6).

The glorious, imperishable, powerful, spiritual bodies all Christians will receive (1 Cor. 15:42–44) will be like the body with which our Lord Jesus rose from the tomb, ministered for forty days to His disciples, and then visibly ascended from their presence into heaven with the angelic promise that He would come back the same way. As Paul explained, "Just as we have borne the likeness of the earthly man, so shall we bear the likeness of the man from heaven" (15:49).

Another difference of interpretation exists over the time of the transla-tion of all Christians in relation to other future events predicted in Scripture, particularly the time of great tribulation on the earth (Matt. 24:21). In the two major passages in which Paul discussed the Rapture (1 Cor. 15:50–58; 1 Thess. 4:13–18), no preceding event or anticipatory sign is mentioned. It is the next specific event in God's program. Therefore, believers are ex-horted to live exemplary lives honoring to God, "while we wait for the blessed hope" (Titus 2:13). Christians are to remember that our "citizenship is in heaven. And we eagerly await a Savior from there, the Lord Jesus Christ" (Phil. 3:20; 1 Cor. 1:7). The belief that the glorified Christ could come for His church at any moment is called the imminent return of Christ. This is the belief that no predicted biblical event must precede it and that, as a result, it could occur at any moment. This has been the belief of many

Christians from New Testament days. This is why Christians are exhorted to "eagerly await" the Lord's coming (Phil. 3:20); their next step might take them heavenward to meet their Lord and Savior.

This teaching is also known as "pretribulationism," the belief that the translation of the church will occur before the Great Tribulation. In addition to being based on the imminency of Christ's coming for His church, however, pretribulationalism also rests on the biblical teaching that "God did not appoint us to suffer wrath but to receive salvation through our Lord Jesus Christ" (1 Thess. 5:9) and that Jesus has rescued us "from the coming wrath" (1:10). The tribulation is the outpouring of God's wrath on a Christ-rejecting world of mankind, designed at least in part to bring the Jewish people to repentance before God (Dan. 12:1; Joel 2:1–18). Thus it has no relationship to the church of Jesus Christ. Most of the other views of the relationship between the translation of the church and the tribulation—midtribulationalism, posttribulationalism, and the recent "pre-wrath rapture" view—compromise in some way or another the biblical teaching of the imminent coming of Christ and of the nature of the tribulation.

An additional view not in accord with the biblical teaching is the partial rapture position. This is a divergent position from pretribulationalism, but it insists that the Rapture is only for Christians "who are watching and waiting for Christ's return. . . . Thus, the *subjects*, not the *timing* of the Rapture is at issue. . . . The Rapture is viewed as a reward, not a privilege." As pretribulationist Paul Lee Tan explains, this position holds that "several groups will be raptured during the Tribulation—as they become spiritually prepared."[3] The Scriptures used to support this view are misinterpreted. For example, Paul's statement, "each in his own turn" (1 Cor. 15:23), in relation to their being resurrected does not indicate divisions in the ranks of believers. Instead it points to what Paul explained in the same verse: "Christ, the firstfruits; then, when he comes, those who belong to him." That is, the sequence is Christ's resurrection and then the resurrection of those who are His. Paul specifically affirmed that Christ "died for us so that, whether we are awake or asleep [spiritually], we may live together with him" (1 Thess. 5:10).

THE JUDGMENT SEAT OF CHRIST
TO REWARD ALL CHRISTIANS

In exhorting the Corinthian Christians to seek to live to please the Lord (2 Cor. 5:9), the apostle Paul reminded them, "For we must all appear before the judgment seat of Christ, that each one may receive what is due him for the things done while in the body, whether good or bad" (5:10). Elsewhere Paul warned the Corinthians about the importance of building properly on the foundation of Jesus Christ. "If any man builds on this foundation using gold, silver, costly stones, wood, hay or straw, his work will be shown for what it is, because the Day will bring it to light. It will be revealed with fire, and the fire will test the quality of each man's work. If what he has built survives, he will receive his reward. If it is burned up, he will suffer loss; he himself will be saved, but only as one escaping through the flames" (1 Cor. 3:12–15).

The Greek word rendered "judgment seat" in 2 Corinthians 5:10 is *bēma*. This is appropriate because in the Greco-Roman world *bēma* was the name for the seat where judges rendered decisions. It is used of Pilate's seat when he delivered Jesus to the Jews for crucifixion (John 19:13). It is translated "court" in Acts 18:12, 16, 17; 25:6, 10, 17. At the judgment seat of Christ He will make decisions or judgments concerning the actions of Christians. However, the *bēma* was also the seat from which awards for various Grecian races and games were distributed. It was in this sense that Paul used the word *bēma*. Earlier Paul had written, "It is the Lord who judges me. Therefore judge nothing before the appointed time; wait till the Lord comes. He will bring to light what is hidden in darkness and will expose the motives of men's hearts. At that time each will receive his praise from God" (1 Cor. 4:4–5). At the judgment seat of Christ no sins will be mentioned since they have been paid for by the death of Jesus, but believers' service will be dealt with on the basis of their motives. The last sentence in the above quotation points to the fact that at the judgment seat of Christ every Christian will receive some reward from the Lord.

THE MARRIAGE OF CHRIST, THE LAMB,
AND HIS BRIDE, THE CHURCH, IN HEAVEN

After the church is translated to heaven, she must pass before the judgment seat of Christ before her marriage to Christ, the Bridegroom. This is because the judgment seat deals with "the things done while in the body, whether good or bad" (2 Cor. 5:10), and at the marriage Christ's bride will have "made herself ready" with fine linen, which depicts "the righteous acts of the saints" (Rev. 19:7–8). The spiritual union between Christ Jesus and the members of His church individually and corporately is so intimate that it is illustrated by a physical body and its head and serves as a model for husbands and wives in Christian marriage (Eph. 5:22–33). This union however, will be consummated when the church is transported to heaven, prepared by the judgment seat, and then finally united forever with Christ, her glorified Lord.

In discussing the marriage of the Lamb it is important to distinguish this both in time and place from the "wedding supper." The angel told John, "Write: 'Blessed are those who are invited to the wedding supper of the Lamb!'" (Rev. 19:9). Jewish weddings normally included three stages. After the parents of the groom paid the dowry (stage one), the groom would go to the bride's home (sometime later, perhaps up to a year) to claim her and take her to his home (stage two; see Matt. 25:1–13). This would be followed by a wedding feast (stage three) that might last for several days (John 2:1–10). In Revelation 19:9 the wedding feast is stage three. The marriage of Christ and the church (stage two) will have already occurred before the feast. One reason for saying this is that in Revelation 19:7 the word "bride" is not the usual word, *nymphē* (John 3:29; Rev. 18:23), but *gynē* (literally, a wife, a married woman). The instruction in Revelation 19:9 for John to write blessings on those invited to the wedding supper suggests that it is a future event that will follow Christ's triumphant return to the earth described in 19:11–19. In the Rapture, Christ will take His bride to Himself. Then when He returns to the earth, He will celebrate this union at a wedding banquet to which saints of other ages will be invited. As John Walvoord observes, "The beginning of the Millennium itself will fulfill the symbolism of the wedding supper (*gamos*)" and "the wedding feast is an earthly feast . . . and thus will take place on earth at the beginning of the Millennium."[4]

The glorified Christ reminds all Christians, "Yes, I am coming soon." And all Christians should respond, "Amen. Come, Lord Jesus" (22:20).

Part 4

THE REIGNING
KING OF GOD

———◉———

Eleven

THE ESTABLISHMENT OF THE REIGN
OF THE KING ON EARTH

———◦◉◦———

W HEN THE LORD JESUS' DISCIPLES during His earthly ministry became convinced He was the Messiah, they anticipated that His establishment of the messianic kingdom would occur momentarily. After all, both John the Baptist and Jesus preached, "Repent, for the kingdom of heaven is near" (Matt. 3:2; 4:17), and, indeed, it was offered to the Jewish people. The disciples' expectation is illustrated by the mother of Zebedee's sons asking Jesus to grant that "one of these two sons of mine may sit at your right and the other at your left in your kingdom" (20:20–21; Mark 10:35–37). As Jesus and His disciples drew near to Jerusalem from Jericho on His final journey, He had told them a number of times of His approaching suffering and death. But still "the people thought that the kingdom of God was going to appear at once" (Luke 19:11).

In an effort to inform His disciples that this was not the case Jesus told the parable of "a man of noble birth" who "went to a distant country to have himself appointed king and then to return" (19:12). The experience of Herod Archelaus, son of Herod the Great, was similar to this. Archelaus went to Rome to secure from Augustus Caesar permission to reign as a client king over a Roman territory.[1] Jesus' parable teaches, of course, the need for Him to suffer and die, to be resurrected and ascend to heaven, where He is now carrying on His ministry to His body, the church, until

147

God the Father will put His enemies under His feet and give Him the kingdom. Progressive dispensationalism, in insisting that Jesus is now reigning in heaven as the Davidic King, does not face the implications of this parable in its obvious application to Jesus in His present ministry in heaven and His return to earth when He will reign as King.

In Jesus' parable, as with Herod Archelaus, the nobleman's "subjects hated him and sent a delegation after him to say, 'We don't want this man to be our king'" (19:14). This paralleled the response of the Jewish leaders and mob when Pilate presented Jesus to them as their King. Not only did they reject Jesus as King but they pressured Pilate to have Him crucified. After His resurrection Jesus' disciples still anticipated the establishment of His messianic kingdom, as seen in their question, "Lord, are you at this time going to restore the kingdom to Israel?" (Acts 1:6). In His response Jesus made it clear God the Father is in charge of the kingdom plans and schedule (1:7; see Matt. 24:36; Mark 13:32). When Christ does return to earth to establish His messianic kingdom, He will take vengeance on His enemies (Rev. 19:11–21), just as Archelaus did when he returned to Judea to rule from 4 B.C. to A.D. 6.[2]

THE TRIBULATION JUDGMENT OF ISRAEL AND THE GENTILES

In this discussion of the tribulation the focus is on the glorified Christ and His involvement in it. First, it is important to see that the judgments of the tribulation as set forth in the "scroll with writing on both sides and sealed with seven seals" (Rev. 5:1) are controlled by "him who sat on the throne." Second, the execution of the judgments is committed to the "Lamb, looking as if it had been slain" (5:6), also identified as "the Lion of the tribe of Judah, the Root of David" (5:5). This is the glorified Christ, who "came and took the scroll from the right hand of him who sat on the throne" (5:7). This is appropriate in view of Jesus' statement during His earthly ministry that "the Father judges no one, but has entrusted all judgment to the Son. . . . And he has given him authority to judge because he is the Son of Man" (John 5:22, 27; see v. 30).

Although the judgments of the tribulation will occur when the glorified Christ is still in heaven, they are discussed here under His future ministry because they relate to the preparation for His return to earth to establish His messianic rule. Responsibility for those judgments rests with Christ because He is the One who will open the scroll's seals (Rev. 5:5), but the judgments themselves will be carried out by angelic agents. The judgments progressively increase in severity, but they are a unitary outpouring of God's judgment on a Christ-rejecting world. No basis exists in the scriptural account to insert either a midtribulational or a so-called pre-wrath Rapture of the church, as some Bible teachers do.

With the opening of the first seal a rider on a white horse "was given a crown, and he rode out as a conqueror bent on conquest" (6:2). This rider may well be the Antichrist, seeking conquest of the world. His efforts will be resisted, so the opening of the second seal reveals a red horse whose rider "was given power to take peace from the earth and to make men slay each other" (6:4). The natural consequence of worldwide conflict was famine, portrayed by the "black horse," with its rider "holding a pair of scales in his hand" (6:5) when the third seal will be opened. This in turn will result in plague and death, represented by the "pale horse" (6:8), when the fourth seal will be opened.

All the conflict and turmoil involved in the opening of the first four seals will result in the death of many "who had been slain because of the word of God and the testimony they had maintained" (6:9). These are revealed with the opening of the fifth seal and are individuals martyred for their faith in God and Christ during the Tribulation (7:14). The results of the opening of the first five seals come from the activities of people with each other, but are all under the control of God and the glorified Christ. With the opening of the sixth seal, however, the judgments will come directly from the Lord through cosmic disturbances (6:12–14). However, instead of repenting and turning to God, unsaved people will hide in caves and will call on the mountains and rocks to fall on them and hide them "from the face of him who sits on the throne and from the wrath of the Lamb! For the great day of their wrath has come, and who can stand?" (6:16–17). Although these judgments will fall on Jews and Gentiles alike, "144,000 from all the tribes of Israel" (7:4–8) will be sealed as servants of God with "a seal on the foreheads" (7:3).

The Thessalonian believers had been enduring "persecutions and trials" (2 Thess. 1:4). These difficulties, coupled with "some prophecy, report or letter supposed to have come from us [Paul], saying that the Day of the Lord has already come" (2:2), alarmed them. Paul, however, indicated that "that day will not come until the rebellion [*apostasia*, apostasy] occurs and the man of lawlessness is revealed, the man doomed to destruction. He will oppose and will exalt himself over everything that is called God or is worshiped, and so that he sets himself up in God's temple, proclaiming himself to be God" (2:3–4). The Day of the Lord, as a result, is identified by specific events. But the Rapture, in which Christ will come to gather His church to Himself—to which Paul referred as a source of encouragement (1 Thess. 4:18)—is not identified by other contemporary happenings. Therefore the Day of the Lord must follow the translation of the church. That "day"[3] includes the "seven years of Tribulation" and, in fact, "the entire period from the beginning of the Tribulation to the end of the millennium."[4]

The opening of the seventh seal (Rev. 8:1) introduces in turn the blowing of seven trumpets by seven angels (8:6), the "seven angels with the seven last plagues" (15:1), and "the seven angels" with "the seven bowls of God's wrath" (16:1). All this marks the completion of God's wrath (15:1), which will be consummated with the destruction of "BABYLON THE GREAT THE MOTHER OF PROSTITUTES" (17:5; see 18:2), the epitome of human independence and opposition to God and Christ. The destruction of Babylon will complete the outpouring of God's wrath and the preparation on earth for the return of the glorified Christ to establish His kingdom.

THE RETURN OF THE KING TO EARTH
IN TRIUMPH OVER HIS ENEMIES

The apostle John described the glorified Christ as a rider "called Faithful and True" seated on "a white horse" (Rev. 19:11). He is not to be confused with the previous rider on "a white horse" (6:2), as some Bible students do; numerous details make the distinction obvious. As Walvoord explains, "the white horse is a symbol of victory. Roman generals after a victory in battle would ride a white horse in triumph with their captives following."[5] This one also is named "the Word of God" (19:13) and "KING OF KINGS AND LORD

OF LORDS" (19:16). He will wear "many crowns" (19:12), He will have "a sharp sword" coming "out of his mouth" (19:15; see 1:16), perhaps symbolizing judgment, and He will be followed by "the armies of heaven . . . riding on white horses and dressed in fine linen, white and clean" (19:14). He will judge "with justice," He will "strike down the nations," and He will tread "the winepress of the fury of God Almighty" (19:11, 15). The fact that "God is love" (1 John 4:16) does not eliminate the necessity for His judgment of His enemies, both angelic and human.

The Judgment of the Beast and the False Prophet

When Christ returns to earth, He will be opposed by "the beast and the kings of the earth and their armies" (Rev. 19:19). This beast is described in Revelation 13:1–8. The dragon, identified as "that ancient serpent called the devil or Satan" (12:9), will give the Beast, the Antichrist, power and authority (13:2), with the result that he will have "authority over every tribe, people, language and nation" (13:7) in the three and a-half years preceding the Second Coming. Paul called this world ruler "the man of lawlessness" (2 Thess. 2:3) and "the lawless one" (2:8–9). "The secret power of lawlessness" that this man will personify "is already at work," but it is now being restrained until "the one who now holds it back . . . is taken out of the way" (2:7). This is most likely the Holy Spirit working in and through the members of Christ's body, the church, whom He indwells and empowers. When the Holy Spirit departs with the church in the Rapture, the lawless one will be free to manifest himself. In the middle of the seven-year Tribulation his identity will be plainly revealed by his setting "himself up in God's temple, proclaiming himself to be God" (2:4).

The apostle John called this person "Antichrist," one who is yet to come (1 John 2:18; see 4:3). But anyone who "denies the Father and the Son" is "the antichrist" (2:22) in attitude. Denying the Godhead is "the spirit of the antichrist," who "is already in the world" (4:3). As a result John wrote, "even now many antichrists have come" (2:18; 2 John 7). Likewise in His Olivet Discourse the Lord Jesus warned the apostles that "many will come in my name, claiming, 'I am the Christ'" (Matt. 24:5) and that "false Christs and false prophets will appear and perform great signs and miracles"

(24:24). He also said "the abomination that causes desolation" will be seen "standing in the holy place" (Matt. 24:15; Mark 13:14; see Dan. 9:27; 11:31; 12:11). This is the Beast, the lawless one, the Antichrist, "whom the Lord Jesus will overthrow with the breath of his mouth and destroy by the splendor of his coming" (2 Thess. 2:8).

Associated with the Beast, who is the Antichrist, is "another beast, coming out of the earth. In John's vision this beast "had two horns like a lamb, but he spoke like a dragon" (Rev. 13:11). This beast will exercise "all the authority of the first beast on his behalf," and will make "the earth and its inhabitants worship the first beast" (13:12; see vv. 14–15). Called the false prophet (16:13), he will be captured by the triumphant Christ together with the Beast and "the two of them" will be thrown into "the fiery lake of burning sulfur" (19:20). The armies they lead will be "killed with the sword that came out of the mouth of the rider on the horse" (19:21).

The Judgment of Living Jews and Gentiles

Although many Jews and believing Gentiles will be martyred in the Great Tribulation during the reign of the Beast (Rev. 12:17; 13:15), a multitude of both groups will still be alive when Christ returns to earth to establish His kingdom. He will examine their qualification to enter the kingdom. This judgment of living Jews is presented by Jesus in two parables in His Olivet Discourse. The first is the parable of the "ten virgins who took their lamps and went out to meet the bridegroom" (Matt. 25:1). The five foolish virgins, who did not take any oil with them (25:3), were not able to welcome the bridegroom when he came or to go with him to the wedding banquet (25:10). When they sought entrance, the bridegroom replied, "I tell you the truth, I don't know you" (25:12).

The second parable is that of a "man going on a journey, who called his servants and entrusted his property to them" (25:14). When he returned, he demanded an accounting. The faithful servants were rewarded with increased responsibilities, but the "worthless servant" was thrown "outside, into the darkness, where there will be weeping and gnashing of teeth" (25:30). This judgment of the Jewish people is predicted in Ezekiel 20:32–44 and Zechariah 13:1.

Many Gentiles will also be alive when the triumphant Christ returns to earth to establish His kingdom. They will be judged on the basis of their faith in Christ, as demonstrated by their treatment of the hunted Jews during the Beast's reign. Just as the ten Boom family and many others, both Christian and non-Christian, befriended and protected Jews during Hitler's regime, Gentiles who in the Tribulation will be trusting Christ and anticipating His return will risk their own lives by befriending Jews. Gentiles will be allowed to enter the kingdom if they have treated Jesus favorably, as represented by their treatment of "the least of these brothers of mine" (Matt. 25:40), that is, "Jews," who are "physical brothers of the Lord."[6] These Gentiles will be invited to "take [their] inheritance, the kingdom prepared for [them] since the creation of the world" (25:34). Unbelieving Gentiles "will go away to eternal punishment, but the righteous to eternal life" (25:46).

The Binding of Satan

Following his victory over Adam and Eve in the Garden of Eden, Satan, represented by the serpent, was told by God that the offspring of the woman in the person of Jesus, the incarnate Son of God, "will crush your head" (Gen. 3:15), signifying total defeat. This was accomplished by Jesus' sacrificial death and resurrection, so that the Holy Spirit now convicts "in regard to judgment, because the prince of this world now stands condemned" (John 16:11). When the seventy-two reported to Jesus, "'Lord, even the demons submit to us in your name,' he replied, 'I saw Satan fall like lightning from heaven'" (Luke 10:17–18). Jesus' response undoubtedly looks ahead to Satan's being "hurled to the earth, and his angels with him" (Rev. 12:9). But it also refers to Satan's power being broken by Jesus' earthly ministry, with Satan being subject to Jesus. Paul encouraged the Roman Christians by writing, "The God of peace will soon crush Satan under your feet" (Rom. 16:20). At the middle of the seven-year Tribulation, there will be "war in heaven," in which Michael and his angels will fight against Satan, the dragon, and he will be "hurled to the earth, and his angels with him" (Rev. 12:7, 9). Then at the beginning of Christ's messianic reign, Satan's activity on the earth will end for a thousand years. When Christ returns to earth, an angel will come down from heaven, with "the key to the Abyss and holding in his hand a great chain." He will bind Satan for a thousand years in the Abyss, and the devil will not be able to deceive the nations any more, until the thousand years are ended (20:1–3). Freedom from demonic and Satanic influence will mark the Lord's millennial kingdom of righteousness and peace.

THE RESURRECTION OF BELIEVING JEWS AND GENTILES

A roster of Old Testament saints—believing Israelites who achieved great feats for God by faith—died without receiving "what had been promised" (Heb. 11:39). Reasons they will not be resurrected with Christians at the return of Christ in the air for the resurrection and translation of church saints have already been discussed. Instead, Old Testament believers will be resurrected at the beginning of the messianic, millennial kingdom of Jesus Christ. Also included in this resurrection will be the Jewish and Gentile martyrs of the Tribulation. John wrote, "I saw the souls of those who had been beheaded because of their testimony for Jesus and because of the word of God. They had not worshiped the beast or his image and had not received his mark on their foreheads or their hands. They came to life and reigned with Christ a thousand years" (Rev. 20:4). When Christ returns to earth the citizens of the messianic kingdom will consist of (a) the church, which will return with Christ from heaven in glorified bodies, (b) resurrected saints from the Old Testament and the Tribulation in glorified bodies, and (c) redeemed Jews and Gentiles who will enter the Millennium in their mortal bodies because of their faith in Christ. All unbelievers and rebels will have been removed, as well as the Beast and the False Prophet, and Satan will have been cast into the Abyss bound in a great chain for the thousand years of the messianic kingdom.

Some Bible teachers believe that a good portion of the thousand years will be occupied in the judgment of living Jews and Gentiles. Divine judgment and justice, however, do not move as slowly nor as imperfectly as some human judicial systems. Christ's judgment may occupy a brief period of time as an interlude between His return to earth and the establishment of the kingdom itself, but the kingdom will include only glorified and living believers in the Lord Jesus Christ.

Twelve

THE ONE-THOUSAND-YEAR REIGN
OF THE KING ON EARTH

———◈———

THE CONSISTENT TEACHING of Scripture is that the Lord Jesus will return from heaven to establish His messianic kingdom on earth in fulfillment of God's promises to Abraham, David, and the people of Israel. The Lord Himself told His apostles that cosmic disturbances will follow the Tribulation and "at that time men will see the Son of Man coming in clouds with great power and glory. And he will send his angels and gather his elect from the four winds, from the ends of the earth to the ends of the heavens" (Mark 13:26–27; see Matt. 24:30–31). The apostles asked the resurrected Jesus if He would "restore the kingdom to Israel" (Acts 1:6), and Peter urged the Jews, "Repent, then, and turn to God . . . that he may send the Christ, who has been appointed for you— even Jesus. He must remain in heaven until the time comes for God to restore everything, as he promised long ago through his holy prophets" (3:19–21). This belief that Christ will return to earth to establish His messianic kingdom on the throne of David for one thousand years is known as premillennialism.

Two other points of view regarding the Millennium are amillennialism and postmillennialism. Amillennialism, which can be traced back at least as far as Augustine, if not to Origen, "holds that the kingdom promises in the Old Testament are fulfilled spiritually rather than literally in the New

155

Testament church." It holds that Christ will literally return to the earth, but it does not believe in His thousand-year reign on the earth. According to amillennarians "the kingdom of God is present in the church age," at the end of which "the second coming of Christ inaugurates the eternal state."[1]

In some respects postmillennialism is a development from amillennialism. Although elements of this view appear earlier, its systematic development is attributed to Daniel Whitby (1638–1725), a Unitarian. Simply stated, it teaches that "Christ's return to earth will occur at the end of the Millennium."[2] The older form of postmillennialism taught that the spread of the gospel of Christ would transform the world system and usher in an era of righteousness and peace, at the end of which Christ will return to inaugurate the eternal state. This view became fairly dominant during the optimistic period of social and industrial progress during the eighteenth, nineteenth, and early twentieth centuries. It was largely abandoned with the worldwide turmoil beginning with World War I. A more contemporary variation is known as "theonomic postmillennialism," which promotes "progress through the church's preaching of the gospel and application of the Mosaic Law" and affirms "the total transformation of culture through the application of biblical law."[3]

ITS FULFILLMENT OF THE OLD TESTAMENT PROMISES TO ISRAEL

The crux of the difference between premillennialism and other points of view is the consistent literal interpretation of Scripture, including Old Testament prophecy. Premillennialism also takes literally the six references to one thousand years in Revelation 20:2–4, 6–7, which both amillennialism and postmillennialism spiritualize. Premillennialism interprets the covenantal promises God made to Abraham, David, and the Jewish people, as well as prophecies related to their fulfillment, as literal promises and prophecies referring to Israel's land and restoration, and an heir, throne, and kingdom.

God's Covenant with Abraham

God's promises to Abraham for his obedience in leaving his country, people, and father's household to go to a land God would show him (Gen. 12:2–3) were certainly fulfilled literally. Later, in a covenant confirmed with animal sacrifices, the Lord said, "To your descendants I give this land, from the river of Egypt to the great river, the Euphrates" (15:18). Still later God confirmed His covenant, changing Abram's name to Abraham and saying, "I will establish my covenant as an everlasting covenant between me and you. . . . The whole land of Canaan, where you are now an alien, I will give as an everlasting possession to you and your descendants after you; and I will be their God" (17:7–8). The sign of circumcision was given as "the sign of the covenant between me and you" (17:11). This covenant was later confirmed with Isaac (26:2–4) and Jacob (28:13–15), and its understanding by the people of Israel is stated in Psalm 105:8–11 and referred to by John the Baptist's mother, Elizabeth (Luke 1:55).

The Palestinian Covenant

Although the term "Palestinian Covenant" is the traditional name for the covenant recorded in Deuteronomy 29–30, perhaps a better title would be Land Covenant, because it deals with the land promised to Abraham and his descendants.[4] After listing "eight specific provisions" of this covenant, Fruchtenbaum concluded, "The special importance of this covenant is that it reaffirmed Israel's title deed to the land. Although Israel would prove unfaithful and disobedient, the right to the land would never be taken from Israel. While her enjoyment of the land is conditioned on obedience, ownership of the land is unconditional. Furthermore, it shows that the conditional Mosaic covenant did not lay aside the unconditional Abrahamic covenant."[5]

Israel's disobedience to the Lord in turning to idols would result in the land being judged (Deut. 29:22–27) and the people dispersed from the land (29:28; 28:64–65). Ezekiel described how God chose Israel to be His child (Ezek. 16:6–7) and later took her to be his cherished wife (16:8–14). Israel, however, was like a spiritual prostitute in that she forsook God to worship idols (16:15–34). As a result God would punish Israel with severe judgments and worldwide dispersion, both of which have occurred since the destruction of the temple and Jerusalem in A.D. 70. The LORD said, however, "Yet I will remember the covenant I made with you in the days of your youth, and I will establish an everlasting covenant with you. . . . So I will establish my covenant with you, and you will know that I am the LORD" (16:59–60, 62).

In view of Ezekiel's prophecy, this land covenant was not fulfilled by the entrance into and conquest of the land under Joshua nor in Israel's time of greatest expansion during Solomon's reign. Yet the covenant assures Israel that when she returns to the Lord and obeys Him wholeheartedly, then the Lord "will restore your fortunes and have compassion on you and gather you again from all the nations where he scattered you. . . . He will bring you to the land that belonged to your fathers, and you will take possession of it" (Deut. 30:2–3, 5). The Old Testament prophets frequently predicted this restoration of Israel to her land (Isa. 11:11–16; 43:5–7; Jer. 16:14–15; 23:3, 7–8; 31:7–11; Ezek. 11:16–17; 36:24, 28; Amos 9:14–15; Zeph. 3:19–20; Zech. 10:8–12). The Lord Jesus confirmed the fulfillment of this land covenant when He told the apostles that at His return the Son of Man "will send his angels with a loud trumpet call, and they will gather his elect from the four winds, from one end of the heavens to the other" (Matt. 24:31; see Mark 13:27). This apparently has begun to occur in the return of Jews to the land and the establishment of the nation of Israel, but the prophecies await complete fulfillment as part of Christ's second coming.

God's Covenant with David

This covenant was announced to David by the prophet Nathan in response to David's desire to build a temple for God in Jerusalem (2 Sam. 7:1–3). God promised that He would "raise up your offspring to succeed you" (7:12), a promise fulfilled in Solomon, who would build a house for God (7:13). God would discipline Solomon for doing wrong, but He would never take His love away from him as He did from Saul (7:14–15). God promised David, "Your house [i.e., lineage] and your kingdom will endure forever before me; your throne will be established forever" (7:16). The account also is found in 1 Chronicles 17:1–15. David described this as "an everlasting covenant, arranged and secured in every part" (2 Sam. 23:5). In addition it is affirmed in Psalm 89:3, 20–37.

Old Testament prophecies identify the fulfillment of this covenant with a future Descendant of David, Israel's Messiah. Isaiah spoke of the Child to be born and the Son to be given, who was obviously a divine person and would "reign on David's throne and over his kingdom, establishing and upholding it with justice and righteousness from that time on and forever" (Isa. 9:6–7; see 11:1–5). Jeremiah spoke of God making "a righteous Branch sprout from David's line" (Jer. 33:15) and indicated that God's covenant with David was as secure as His covenant with day and night (33:17–22; see 23:5–6). The angel Gabriel identified the Virgin Mary's Spirit-conceived Son, Jesus, as the One to whom "the Lord God will give . . . the throne of his father David, and he will reign over the house of Jacob forever; his kingdom will never end" (Luke 1:32–33). This will be fulfilled when Christ returns to earth in triumph and great glory.

Promises to the People of Israel

The promises to the people of Israel concerning restoration to fellowship with God in the messianic kingdom obviously are related to the fulfillment of the Abrahamic, Land, and Davidic covenants, but they also are directly related to the people. God told Israel through Moses, "For you are a people holy to the LORD your God. The LORD your God has chosen you out of all the peoples on the face of the earth to be his people, his treasured possession" (Deut. 7:6; 14:2; see Ps. 135:4). After calling the "sons of Jacob" God's "chosen ones" (Ps. 105:6), the psalmist stated that God "remembers his covenant forever, the word he commanded, for a thousand generations" (105:8).

Because Israel has turned away from God in disobedience and rebellion, God has had to discipline His chosen people with dispersion throughout the world and with severe hardships and trials. However, He declared to Israel, "I have chosen you and have not rejected you. So do not fear, for I am with you; do not be dismayed, for I am your God" (Isa. 41:9–10; see 43:1; 44:1–2). The apostle Paul emphasized the permanence of God's choice of the Israelites when he wrote, "Did God reject his people?

By no means! . . . God did not reject his people, whom he foreknew" (Rom. 11:1–2). Paul proved this by stating that God is now saving Israelites like Paul by having them respond to the gospel of Christ and become members of His body, the church, and by stating that in the future messianic kingdom "all Israel will be saved" (11:26; see Dan. 12:1). All this is true because "God's gifts and his call are irrevocable" (Rom. 11:29).

THE INHABITANTS OF THE MILLENNIAL KINGDOM

After the Lord judges the Israelites at the beginning of the Millennium to purge "those who revolt and rebel" against Him (Ezek. 20:38), the believing remnant of Israel will be brought "into the bond of the covenant" (20:37). They will be living citizens of the millennial, messianic kingdom of the Lord Jesus Christ. In addition the saints of the Old Testament will be resurrected to be citizens of the kingdom (Isa. 26:19; Ezek. 37:12–14). So also the tribulation martyrs, both Jews and Gentiles, will be resurrected to enter the millennial kingdom as the Lord's citizens. The kingdom inhabitants will also include the body and bride of Christ, His church resurrected and transformed before the Tribulation, which will return with Him. Thus at the beginning of the messianic kingdom every inhabitant will be a redeemed, believing person, either perfected through resurrection or transformation, or a living believer among the Jews or Gentiles.

Since the Lord Jesus Christ will be reigning as Israel's Messiah on the throne of David, the people of Israel will be "the head, not the tail" (Deut. 28:13) among the nations. Furthermore, Israel will be a united nation once again instead of being divided into Judah and Israel (Ezek. 37:15–28). Jerusalem will be the political capital of the world as the city from which Christ will reign on David's throne (Jer. 33:14–18); it will also be the spiritual center with a rebuilt temple for the worship of God (Isa. 2:1–3; 62:1–7; Mic. 4:1–3; Zech. 14:10–11, 16–17, 20–21). The redeemed people of Israel "will be called the priests of the LORD . . . ministers of our God" (Isa. 61:6).

The general teaching of the Old Testament (Ps. 132:10–11; Isa. 9:6–7; Jer. 33:17, 20–21) and the belief of the Jews was that the Messiah would fulfill God's promise to David that one of his descendants would restore his kingdom and sit on his throne. This was the angel Gabriel's promise to Mary concerning Jesus (Luke 1:31–33), it is what Jesus taught (Matt. 19:28), and it is what the disciples believed (Matt. 20:21; Acts 1:6). A question arises, however, concerning the place in the millennial kingdom of the resurrected David, especially in light of some prophecies that speak of him as a millennial ruler (Jer. 30:9; Ezek. 34:23–24; 37:24–25; Hos. 3:5). Some Bible students conclude that David will be the actual ruler, but others correctly teach that he will be a co-regent with the glorified Lord Jesus Christ. This is supported by Ezekiel's calling him a "prince" (Ezek. 34:24; 37:25).

THE WORLDWIDE EXTENT
OF THE MILLENNIAL KINGDOM

Although the land that was promised to Israel to be occupied during the millennium was said to be "from the river of Egypt to the great river, the Euphrates—the land of the Kenites, Kenizzites, Kadmonites, Hittites, Perizzites, Rephaites, Amorites, Canaanites, Girgashites and Jebusites" (Gen. 15:18–21), the dominion of the messianic kingdom will be worldwide over all the inhabitants of the earth. This is stated by Isaiah. "In the last days the mountain of the LORD's temple will be established as chief among the mountains; it will be raised above the hills, and all nations will stream to it" (Isa. 2:2). And "the nations will rally to [the Root of Jesse]" (11:10; see 24:14–16; 42:10–13). This worldwide rule is also demonstrated by the Lord's ability to "gather the exiles of Israel" and to "assemble the scattered people of Judah from the four quarters of the earth" (11:12; see v. 11; 66:20; Matt. 24:30–33), for this will be possible only if His authority is worldwide. All other efforts at a worldwide government throughout history have failed and will fail. This includes the United Nations of our present time and the tyrannical reign of the Beast during the Tribulation.

THE CHARACTER OF THE MILLENNIAL KINGDOM

Scripture indicates that Christ's millennial reign will be marked by the worship of God and the qualities of peace, justice, and righteousness. In that time, "Many peoples will come and say, 'Come, let us go up to the mountain of the LORD, to the house of the God of Jacob. He will teach us his ways, so that we may walk in his paths.' The law will go out from Zion, the word of the LORD from Jerusalem" (Isa. 2:3; Mic. 4:2; see Zech. 14:16–21).

If one thing has marked the recorded history of the world, it is the almost continuous pattern of warfare, bloodshed, and death. In the messianic kingdom, however, "They will beat their swords into plowshares and their spears into pruning hooks. Nation will not take up sword against nation, nor will they train for war anymore" (Isa. 2:4; Mic. 4:3). Isaiah also wrote, "They will neither harm nor destroy on all my holy mountain, for the earth will be full of the knowledge of the LORD as the waters cover the sea" (Isa. 11:9). This cessation of conflict and warfare will be because Messiah "will judge between the nations, and will settle disputes for many peoples" (2:4).

The Messiah's judgments and decisions will be carried out, resulting in peace not only because He has the power to enforce His decisions but also because they are equitable and just. His "reign on David's throne and over his kingdom" will be marked by "establishing and upholding it with justice and righteousness from that time on and forever" (9:7). This is because "the Spirit of the LORD will rest on him—the Spirit of wisdom and understanding, the Spirit of counsel and of power, the Spirit of knowledge and of the fear of the LORD" (11:2). As a result, "He will not judge by what he sees with his eyes, or decide by what he hears with his ears; but with righteousness he will judge the needy, with justice he will give decisions for the poor of the earth" (11:3–4). Righteousness and faithfulness will so thoroughly characterize His reign that those qualities are likened to a belt and sash (11:5). As a result, each family will enjoy peace and prosperity, for each one will have his own vineyard and fig tree (Mic. 4:4; Zech. 3:10).

Satan will be bound and cast into the Abyss at the beginning of the Millennium (Rev. 20:1–3), so that the evil influences of him and his demonic forces will no longer impact the living believers entering the kingdom. But those individuals without resurrected bodies, and children born to them, will be mortal human beings with an Adamic nature and the need to trust the Lord Jesus Christ as their Savior. Though the prospects of those children trusting the Lord and being saved will be greater than today, undoubtedly some will remain unsaved, especially as the thousand years go on. As a result, some will rebel against Messiah's rule and will require the punitive judgment of the Lord (Isa. 11:4).

THE TRANSFORMED NATURAL WORLD
OF THE MILLENNIAL KINGDOM

When Adam and Eve succumbed to the temptation of the serpent and sinned by eating the fruit of "the tree of knowledge of good and evil" (Gen. 2:16–17; 3:1–7), God judged the natural order of creation (3:17–19) as well as the serpent (3:14–15), Eve (3:16), and Adam. Everything God had created originally "was very good" (1:31), and the Garden of Eden in which Adam and Eve were placed as custodians was a paradise (2:8–9, 15, 20–25), but it was cursed by their sin. Paul stated, "We know that the whole creation has been groaning as in the pains of childbirth right up to the present time" (Rom. 8:22). It is appropriate, therefore, that the redemption of the human race in the millennial kingdom will also involve, at least in part, the restoration of the pristine state of the created world. Paul declared, "The creation waits in eager expectation for the sons of God to be revealed. For the creation was subjected to frustration, not by its own choice, but by the will of the one who subjected it, in hope that the creation itself will be liberated from its bondage to decay and brought into the glorious freedom of the children of God" (8:19–21). Although the total restoration of God's original creation will not occur until God creates "new heavens and a new earth" (Isa. 65:17; 66:22; 2 Pet. 3:13; Rev. 21:1), Scripture predicts great improvements will be made on the earth in the millennial kingdom of the Messiah.

The first step in the transformation of the natural world will occur with the return of Jesus Christ to the earth. Just as He ascended to God's right hand in heaven from the Mount of Olives (Acts 1:11–12), so He will return to earth to the same spot. "It will be split in two from east to west, forming a great valley, with half of the mountain moving north and half moving south" (Zech. 14:4). Furthermore, "On that day living water will flow out from Jerusalem, half to the eastern sea [the Euphrates River] and half to the western sea [the Mediterranean Sea], in summer and in winter" (14:8; see Ezek. 47:1–12).

In the millennial kingdom the land of Israel will experience greatly increased fertility and productivity of crops. As Amos predicted, "The days are coming . . . when the reaper will be overtaken by the plowman and the planter by the one treading grapes. New wine will drip from the mountains and flow from all the hills" (Amos 9:13; see Isa. 35:1–2, 6–7; 51:3; 55:12–13; Ezek. 34:27; 36:29–30, 34–35; Joel 3:18). To some degree this will be the result of ample rainfall at needed times (Isa. 30:23–26), but it will also result from altered topography of the land of Israel at the beginning of the millennial kingdom, as indicated by the "forming [of] a great valley" (Zech. 14:4) when Mount Olivet divides (see Isa. 35:1–2, 6–7; 41:18–20; 65:12–13). The most complete description of these changes is found in Ezekiel 47:1–12.

Another significant facet of the millennial kingdom will be a greatly increased human lifespan. Isaiah wrote, "Never again will there be in it an infant who lives but a few days, or an old man who does not live out his years; he who dies at a hundred will be thought a mere youth; he who fails to reach a hundred will be considered accursed" (Isa. 65:20). "For as the days of a tree, so will be the days of my people; my chosen ones will long enjoy the works of their hands" (65:22). Although Isaiah opened this section with the words, "I will create new heavens and a new earth" (65:17), he must have been talking about the millennial kingdom, because he spoke of death, which will not occur in the eternal state (1 Cor. 15:21; Rev. 21:4).

A final evidence of the transformation of the natural order will be the removal of the carnivorous and poisonous natures from all wild animals. Isaiah predicted, "The wolf will live with the lamb, the leopard will lie down with the goat, the calf and the lion and the yearling together; and a little child will lead them. The cow will feed with the bear, their young will lie down together, and the lion will eat straw like the ox. The infant will play near the hole of the cobra, and the young child put his hand into the viper's nest" (Isa. 11:6–8). God promised at that time to "make a covenant of peace with them and rid the land of wild beasts" (Ezek. 34:25; see Hos. 2:18).

Truly the earth will enjoy millennial peace, beauty, and productivity. At least in a partial sense the world will be redeemed when Jesus Christ, the Messiah, rules on earth as the sovereign King in the millennial kingdom.

Thirteen

THE CONSUMMATION OF THE
REIGN OF THE KING ON EARTH

THE OBJECTIVE OF THIS BOOK has been to point out that the eternal plan of the triune Godhead has been to exalt the eternal Word, the Lord Jesus Christ, as the member of the Godhead who became incarnate to carry out God's program of redemption and salvation (Col. 1:18). This exaltation will be manifested in the messianic millennial kingdom but will not reach its climax until that reign ends and Christ "has destroyed all dominion, authority and power. For he must reign until he has put all his enemies under his feet" (1 Cor. 15:24–25). When God the Father "has put everything under his [Christ's] feet" (15:27), then Christ will hand "over the kingdom to God the Father" (15:24).

The fact that "the last enemy to be destroyed is death" (15:26) demonstrates that the millennial kingdom itself is not the consummation of God's program, because physical death will occur during the millennium (Isa. 65:20). The living believers who will enter the messianic kingdom will be saved because of their faith in Christ, but they will not be perfected. Therefore they will be subject to physical death. Furthermore, during the millennium children born to them will have the Adamic sin nature and will need to exercise faith in the reigning Christ. Undoubtedly many will do so, but those who do not will be judged with the sentence of death, because Christ will rule "with an iron scepter" (Rev. 2:27; 12:5; 19:15).

Physical death, therefore, which will continue through the Millennium, will be eliminated only at the end of the Millennium. This is also why the millennial kingdom is only a partial restoration of the pristine conditions of both humanity and the natural order in the Garden of Eden before the fall of Adam and Eve.

SATAN'S FINAL REBELLION AND JUDGMENT

Throughout the millennial kingdom Satan will be bound and imprisoned in the Abyss "to keep him from deceiving the nations," but at the end of the thousand years he will be "set free for a short time to deceive the nations" (Rev. 20:3, 7–8). This rebellion will serve two purposes. First, it will identify those human beings who will remain unregenerate and will merely be conforming outwardly to the Messiah's authority. After all, people will never have enjoyed such prosperity, abundance of food, and absence of violence and warfare. Satan's deception will lead them to reveal their true character. Second, the rebellion will demonstrate Satan's continued desire to "make myself like the Most High" (Isa. 14:14; see 2 Thess. 2:4). This lay behind the serpent's temptation of Eve, the devil's temptation of Jesus in the desert, and Satan's empowerment and motivation of the "man of lawlessness" (2:3–4, 9). His release from the Abyss to lead the unregenerate at the end of the Millennium into rebellion against Messiah, God's people, and Jerusalem (the city God loves, Rev. 20:9) will be his final effort to achieve his goal. It is doomed to fail as have all his other efforts, for fire will devour his human followers and he will be "thrown into the lake of burning sulfur, where the beast and false prophet," his Tribulation accomplices, "had been thrown" (20:9–10; see 19:20–21). There "they will be tormented day and night for ever and ever" (20:10).

The fact that the millennial kingdom will end in a revolt of citizens who have not responded in saving faith to the reigning Messiah has a tremendous lesson for political and social leaders today. Important as education, environment, and example are in directing young people to becoming productive and successful adults, those factors are not the ultimate criteria. What is important is what is in the heart of the individual. In the Millennium "the earth will be full of the knowledge of the LORD as the waters cover the sea" (Isa. 11:9). All satanic and demonic temptation will be eliminated, and crime and violence will not exist. The environment will be almost perfect and the advantages abundant. The Savior Himself will reign as Messiah, and perfected and living saints will inhabit the earth. In spite of all these positive motivations, multitudes will remain unregenerate, refusing to believe in Christ, and will follow Satan's deception in rebellion against the Messiah.

THE RESURRECTION AND GREAT WHITE THRONE JUDGMENT OF ALL UNBELIEVING DEAD

"Since death came through a man, the resurrection of the dead comes also through a man" (1 Cor. 15:21). This is physical resurrection to physical life, whether as a saved individual in an eternal, spiritual body (15:42–45) or as an unregenerate person subject to judgment and eternal separation from God in torment (2 Pet. 3:7). Both physical and spiritual death came to the human race as a result of sin, specifically disobedience to God's command not to eat the fruit of "the tree of the knowledge of good and evil" (Gen. 2:16–17; 3:6). Adam and Eve's spiritual death is seen in their hiding from God's presence in the Garden (3:8), and in due time they died physically. As Paul claimed, "As in Adam all die, so in Christ all will be made alive" (1 Cor. 15:22), that is, physically alive.

Paul also stated the order of resurrection: "Christ, the firstfruits; then, when he comes, those who belong to him" (15:23). This "first resurrection" (Rev. 20:5–6) consists of two parts: the resurrection of dead Christians at the translation of Christ's body, the church (1 Thess. 4:14–17), and the resurrection of all remaining believers (Old Testament saints and Tribulation martyrs) when Christ returns to earth to establish His millennial kingdom. The last step in the order of resurrection is "the second resurrection," when "the end will come" (1 Cor. 15:24). This is the resurrection of all unbelieving dead. John recorded that "the sea gave up the dead that were in it, and death and Hades gave up the dead that were in them" (Rev. 20:13).

This resurrection is to judgment. John saw "the dead, great and small, standing before the throne," and "the dead were judged according to what they had done as recorded in the books" (20:12). This would suggest that there are degrees of eternal torment for unbelievers, but there is no escape. Together with the books out of which the unbelievers will be judged in this Great White Throne judgment, another book will be opened, "which is the book of life" (20:12). Apparently this book is opened to prove that all the unbelieving dead properly belong before this tribunal, because "if anyone's name was not found written in the book of life, he [will be] thrown into the lake of fire" (20:15). The book of life records only the names of believers (21:27; 13:8; Phil. 4:3).

The Judge who sits on the Great White Throne to pronounce judgment on the resurrected unbelievers is the Lord Jesus Christ. Jesus told the Jews, "Moreover, the Father judges no one, but has entrusted all judgment to the Son, that all may honor the Son just as they honor the Father" (John 5:22–23). God has "given him authority to judge because he is the Son of Man" (5:27). Jesus also said His "judgment is just, for I seek not to please myself but him who sent me" (5:30). What regret and remorse will fill the hearts of unbelievers who stand before the One whose provision of salvation and eternal life they spurned to be condemned to separation from God in the lake of fire for eternity.

THE TRANSFER OF AUTHORITY
TO GOD THE FATHER

With the completion of Christ's ministry with the resurrection and judgment of the unbelieving dead and the consignment of death and Hades to the lake of fire (Rev. 20:14), Christ will hand over "the kingdom to God the Father" (1 Cor. 15:24). When this is accomplished, "then the Son himself will be made subject to him [God the Father] who put everything under him, so that God [the triune Godhead] may be all in all" (15:28). The objective of all that the eternal Word has done in carrying out the eternal plan of God for mankind and the world is expressed in the angel's command to John, "Worship God!" (Rev. 19:10; 22:9).

THE NEW HEAVENS AND NEW
EARTH IN THE ETERNAL STATE

A number of Scriptures state that the present heavens and earth will be removed and new heavens and a new earth created. In His Olivet Discourse the Lord Jesus said, "Heaven and earth will pass away, but my words will never pass away" (Matt. 24:35). The psalmist wrote, "In the beginning you laid the foundations of the earth, and the heavens are the work of your hands. They will perish, but you remain; they will all wear out like a garment. Like clothing you will change them and they will be discarded. But you remain the same, and your years will never end" (Ps. 102:25–27; see Heb. 1:10–12). Also Peter predicted, "The heavens will disappear with a roar; the elements will be destroyed by fire, and the earth and everything in it will be laid bare" (2 Pet. 3:10; see vv. 7, 12). Peter also wrote, "But in keeping with his promise we are looking forward to a new heaven and a new earth, the home of righteousness" (3:13; see Isa. 66:22). This is described in Revelation 21:1–22:5. While some scholars say the heavens and the earth will be renovated, Peter's words seem to suggest that they will be completely destroyed and then replaced with newly created heavens and earth.

The eternal state will include the provision of a new city of Jerusalem for redeemed people (21:9–27). In the eternal state "the dwelling of God is with men, and he will live with them. They will be his people, and God himself will be with them and be their God" (21:3). No temple will be in the New Jerusalem "because the Lord God Almighty and the Lamb are its temple" (21:22). Its citizens will be "only those whose names are written in the Lamb's book of life" (21:27).

CONCLUSION

In view of what the Lord Jesus has done, is doing, and will do, as presented in the Scriptures and discussed in this book, how should we as Christians respond? First, we should praise God for His grace in providing salvation and eternal life through faith in the sacrificial death of the Lord Jesus. Second, because of our position in Christ as members of His body, we should set our minds "on things above, not on earthly things" (Col. 3:2), because our "citizenship is in heaven" (Phil. 3:20). Third, we ought to lead holy lives. When Peter asked, "What kind of people ought you to be?" (2 Pet. 3:11), he responded, "You ought to live holy and godly lives," and he exhorted believers to "make every effort to be found spotless, blameless and at peace with him" (3:14). Fourth, we should live in the hope of our Lord's imminent coming to translate us into His presence (1 Thess. 4:13–18) and after that to return to earth to establish His messianic kingdom. He has promised, "Yes, I am coming soon," and the believer's response should be "Amen. Come, Lord Jesus" (Rev. 22:20).

Endnotes

CHAPTER 1—THE WORD OF GOD AS A MEMBER OF THE TRIUNE GODHEAD

1. G. W. Bromiley, "Word, Word of the Lord," in *Zondervan Pictorial Encyclopedia of the Bible,* ed. Merrill C. Tenney and Steven Barabas (Grand Rapids: Zondervan, 1975), 5:959.

2. Gordon H. Clark, *Thales to Dewey* (Boston: Houghton Mifflin Co., 1957), 19.

3. Ibid., 161.

4. Philip Schaff, *Apostolic Christianity A.D. 1–100,* vol. 1 of *History of the Christian Church* (New York: Scribner's Sons, 1882), 553–54.

5. Marvin R. Vincent, *Word Studies in the New Testament* (New York: Scribner's Sons, 1871), 1:458.

6. E. C. Colwell, "A Definite Rule for the Use of the Article in the Greek New Testament," *Journal of Biblical Literature* 52 (1933): 20.

7. A. T. Robertson, *A Grammar of the Greek New Testament in Light of Historical Research,* 5th ed. (New York: Harper & Brothers, 1923), 417.

8. Merrill C. Tenney, "John," in *Zondervan NIV Bible Commentary,* ed. Kenneth L. Barker and John Kohlenberger III (Grand Rapids: Zondervan, 1994), 2:296.

9. Quoted by Charles Hodge, *Systematic Theology* (New York: Scribner's, 1871; reprint, Grand Rapids: Baker, 1970), 1:458.

10. Ralph L. Woods, ed., *The World Treasury of Religious Quotations* (New York: Hawthorn, 1966), 1000.

11. Quoted in *Quotations for the Christian World*, ed. Edythe Draper (Wheaton, Ill.: Tyndale, 1992), 623.

12. A. T. Robertson, *Word Pictures in the New Testament* (New York: Harper & Brothers, 1930), 4:478–79.

CHAPTER 2—THE PREINCARNATE MINISTRY OF THE WORD OF GOD

1. John F. Walvoord, *Jesus Christ Our Lord* (Chicago: Moody, 1969), 52.

2. Ibid., 54.

CHAPTER 3—THE OLD TESTAMENT ANTICIPATION OF THE INCARNATION OF THE WORD OF GOD

1. Allen P. Ross, "Psalms," in *The Bible Knowledge Commentary, Old Testament*, ed. John F. Walvoord and Roy B. Zuck (Wheaton, Ill.: Victor, 1985), 792.

2. Ibid., 804 (italics his).

3. Ibid., 809.

4. Ibid.

5. John F. Walvoord, *The Prophecy Knowledge Handbook* (Wheaton, Ill.: Victor, 1990), 96.

6. D. F. Payne, "Typology, Biblical," in *New International Dictionary of the Christian Church*, ed. J. D. Douglas (Grand Rapids: Zondervan, 1974), 990.

7. Wick Broomall, "Type, Typology," in *Baker's Dictionary of Theology*, ed. Everett F. Harrison (Grand Rapids: Baker, 1960), 534.

8. Robertson, *Word Pictures* 6:119–20.

9. Roger M. Raymer, "1 Peter," in *The Bible Knowledge Commentary, New Testament*, ed. John F. Walvoord and Roy B. Zuck (Wheaton, Ill.: Victor, 1983), 852.

CHAPTER 4—THE NAMES AND TITLES OF THE SON OF GOD

1. Edwin C. Blum, "John," in *The Bible Knowledge Commentary, New Testament,* 303.
2. Ibid., 301.
3. G. Abbott-Smith, *A Manual Greek Lexicon of the New Testament* (Edinburgh: Clark, 1937), 340 (italics his).
4. Roy B. Zuck, *Teaching as Jesus Taught* (Grand Rapids: Baker, 1995), 42–43.
5. Abbott-Smith, *A Manual Greek Lexicon,* 62.

CHAPTER 5—THE INCARNATION OF THE SON OF GOD ANNOUNCED

1. C. S. Lewis, *Mere Christianity,* rev. and enlarged ed. (New York: Macmillan, 1952), 36.
2. Luke Timothy Johnson, *The Real Jesus* (San Francisco: Harper, 1996), 1.
3. Robert B. Strimple, *The Modern Search for the Real Jesus* (Phillipsburg, N.J.: P & R, 1995), 9.
4. Robert W. Funk, Roy W. Hoover, Jesus Seminar, eds., *The Five Gospels: In Search of the Authentic Jesus* (New York: Macmillan, 1993), 5.
5. Ibid., 16.
6. Ibid.
7. Ibid., 32.
8. Johnson, *The Real Jesus,* v.
9. Ibid., 18.
10. Ibid., 4.
11. Ibid., 6.
12. Ibid., 8.
13. Ibid., 141.
14. W. White, Jr., "Star of the Magi," in *Zondervan Pictorial Encyclopedia of the Bible,* 5:513.
15. Ibid.

CHAPTER 6—THE PERSON OF THE INCARNATE SON OF GOD

1. Charles C. Ryrie, *Basic Theology* (Wheaton, Ill.: Victor, 1986), 247.
2. John F. Walvoord, *Jesus Christ Our Lord* (Chicago: Moody, 1969), 106.
3. Ryrie, *Basic Theology,* 252.
4. "Monarchianism," in *Oxford Dictionary of the Christian Church,* ed. F. L. Cross (London: Oxford University Press, 1957), 914.
5. Ibid.
6. "Arianism," in *Oxford Dictionary of the Christian Church,* 80.
7. Charles Taze Russell, *Studies in the Scriptures* (Brooklyn, N. Y.: Watchtower Bible and Tract Society, 1886), 5:84.
8. James E. Talmadge, *The Philosophical Basis of Mormonism* (Independence, Mo.: Zion's Printing and Publishing, 1915), 7.
9. Hodge, *Systematic Theology,* 2:457.
10. Ibid.
11. Ryrie, *Basic Theology,* 250.
12. Source unknown.
13. Source unknown.
14. Lewis Sperry Chafer, *Systematic Theology* (Dallas: Dallas Seminary Press, 1948; reprint [8 vols. in 4], Grand Rapids: Kregel, 1993), 1:369.

CHAPTER 7—THE EARTHLY LIFE AND MINISTRY OF THE SON OF GOD

1. Robertson, *Word Pictures, 2:32.*
2. Harold W. Hoehner, *Chronological Aspects of the Life of Christ* (Grand Rapids: Zondervan, 1977), 37.
3. Chafer, *Systematic Theology,* 5:101.
4. Charles C. Ryrie, *The Ryrie Study Bible (NASV)* (Chicago: Moody, 1978), 1973.
5. Henry C. Thiessen, "An Outline of Lectures in Systematic Theology," 3d ed. (unpublished class notes, Wheaton College, 1942).
6. *The NIV Study Bible* (Grand Rapids: Zondervan, 1985), 1621.

CHAPTER 8—CHRIST'S ASCENSION TO THE RIGHT HAND OF GOD THE FATHER

1. Ryrie, *The Ryrie Study Bible (NASB)*, 1932.
2. Ibid.

CHAPTER 9—CHRIST'S PRESENT MINISTRY AT THE RIGHT HAND OF GOD THE FATHER

1. Craig A. Blaising and Darrell L. Bock, *Progressive Dispensationalism* (Wheaton, Ill.: Victor, 1993), 49 (italics theirs).
2. Darrell L. Bock, "The Reign of the Lord Christ," in *Dispensationalism, Israel and the Church,* ed. Craig A. Blaising and Darrell L. Bock (Grand Rapids: Zondervan, 1992), 65.
3. Ibid.
4. Ibid., 50.
5. Craig A. Blaising and Darrell L. Bock, "Dispensationalism, Israel and the Church: Assessment and Dialogue," in *Dispensationalism, Israel and the Church*, 381.
6. Ibid. (italics theirs).
7. Ibid., 65.
8. Blaising and Bock, *Progressive Dispensationalism*, 31.
9. Ibid., 152.
10. Ibid.
11. Elliott E. Johnson, "Hermeneutical Principles and the Interpretation of Psalm 110," *Bibliotheca Sacra* 149 (October–December 1992): 433–34 (italics his).
12. Ibid., 436.
13. Abbott-Smith, *A Manual Greek Lexicon*, 340 (italics his).
14. Edwin A. Blum, "John" in *The Bible Knowledge Commentary, New Testament*, 328.

CHAPTER 10—CHRIST'S TRANSLATION OF HIS CHURCH TO HEAVEN

1. Merrill C. Tenney, "John," in *Zondervan NIV Bible Commentary*, 345.
2. Robertson, *Word Pictures*, 5:249.

3. Paul Lee Tan, "Rapture, Partial," in *Dictionary of Premillennial Theology*, ed. Mal Couch (Grand Rapids: Kregel, 1996), 347–48 (italics his).

4. John F. Walvoord, "Revelation," in *The Bible Knowledge Commentary, New Testament*, 975.

CHAPTER 11—THE ESTABLISHMENT OF THE REIGN OF THE KING ON EARTH

1. Walter L. Liefeld, "Luke," in *Zondervan NIV Bible Commentary, New Testament*, ed. Kenneth L. Barker and John Kohlengberger III (Grand Rapids: Zondervan, 1994), 272.

2. Harold W. Hoehner, "Herod," in *Zondervan Pictorial Encyclopedia of the Bible*, 3:138.

3. Arnold G. Fruchtenbaum, "Day of the Lord," in *Dictionary of Premillennial Theology*, 87.

4. Paul Enns, *The Moody Handbook of Theology* (Chicago: Moody, 1986), 633; see 129.

5. John F. Walvoord, "Revelation," in *The Bible Knowledge Commentary, New Testament*, 947; see 976.

6. Louis A. Barbieri, Jr., "Matthew," in *The Bible Knowledge Commentary, New Testament*, 81.

CHAPTER 12—THE ONE-THOUSAND-YEAR REIGN OF THE KING ON EARTH

1. Rick Bowman and Russell L. Penney, "Amillennialism," in *Dictionary of Premillennial Theology*, 37.

2. Thomas D. Ice, "Postmillennialism," in *Dictionary of Premillennial Theology*, 307.

3. Ibid.

4. Arnold Fruchtenbaum, "Palestinian Covenant," in *Dictionary of Premillennial Theology*, 291.

5. Ibid., 291–92.

Bibliography

Berkouwer, G. C. *The Person of Christ.* Grand Rapids: Wm. B. Eerdmans Publishing Co., 1947.

Briner, Bob. *The Management Methods of Jesus.* Nashville: Thomas Nelson, 1996.

Chafer, Lewis Sperry. *Systematic Theology.* Dallas: Dallas Seminary Press, 1948; reprint (8 vols. in 4), Grand Rapids: Kregel Publications, 1993.

Couch, Mal, ed. *Dictionary of Premillennial Theology.* Grand Rapids: Kregel Publications, 1996.

Elwell, Walter A., ed. *A Topical Analysis of the Bible.* Grand Rapids: Baker Books, 1991.

Enns, Paul. *The Moody Handbook of Theology.* Chicago: Moody Press, 1989.

Gariepy, Henry. *100 Portraits of Christ.* Wheaton, Ill.: Victor Books, 1987.

Henry, Carl F. H. *God, Revelation, and Authority.* Vols. 2 and 3. Waco, Tex.: Word Books, 1976, 1979.

Hodge, Charles. *Systematic Theology.* 3 vols. New York: Charles Scribner's, 1911.

Hoehner, Harold W. *Chronological Aspects of the Life of Christ.* Grand Rapids: Zondervan Publishing House, 1977.

Ice, Thomas, and Timothy Demy, eds. *When the Trumpet Sounds.* Eugene, Oreg.: Harvest House Publications, 1995.

Lucado, Max. *No Wonder They Call Him Savior.* Portland, Oreg.: Multnomah Press, 1986.

Morgan, G. Campbell. *The Crises of the Christ*. Westwood, N.J.: Fleming H. Revell Co., 1936.

Pentecost, J. Dwight. *The Words and Works of Jesus Christ*. Grand Rapids: Zondervan Publishing House, 1961.

Ryrie, Charles C. *Basic Theology*. Wheaton, Ill.: Victor Books, 1986.

Schilder, K. *Christ in His Suffering*. Translated by Henry Zylstra. Grand Rapids: Wm. B. Eerdmans Publishing Co., 1938.

_____. *Christ on Trial*. Grand Rapids: Wm. B. Eerdmans Publishing Co., 1939.

_____. *Christ on the Cross*. Grand Rapids: Wm. B. Eerdmans Publishing Co., 1940.

Showers, Renald E. *There Really Is a Difference: A Comparison of Covenant and Dispensational Theology*. Bellmawr, N.J.: Friends of Israel Gospel Ministry, 1990.

Walvoord, John F. *Jesus Christ Our Lord*. Chicago: Moody Press, 1969.

_____. *The Prophecy Knowledge Handbook*. Wheaton, Ill.: Victor Books, 1990.

_____, and Zuck, Roy B., eds. *The Bible Knowledge Commentary*. 2 vols. Wheaton, Ill.: Victor Books, 1983, 1985.

Wells, David F. *The Person of Christ*. Westchester, Ill.: Crossway Books, 1984.

Zuck, Roy B., ed. *Vital Christology Issues*. Grand Rapids: Kregel Publications, 1997.

_____. *Vital Prophecy Issues*. Grand Rapids: Kregel Publications, 1995.

Scripture Index

Subject Index